Reclaiming Eros

SECOND EDITION
Revised and Expanded

Reclaiming Eros

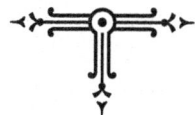

Suzanne Blackburn

FOREWORD BY
Kenneth Ray Stubbs

☾
Blue Moon Books

PORTLAND, MAINE

RECLAIMING EROS

Revised and expanded second edition
Copyright © 2011 by author, Suzanne Blackburn
Published by Blue Moon Books, Portland, Maine,
under the title *Reclaiming Eros*

Original Copyright © 2007 by Suzanne Blackburn and Margaret Wade
Published by Suade Publishing, Portland, Maine,
under the title *Reclaiming Eros: Sacred Whores and Healers*

All rights reserved. No part of this book may be reprinted or used in any form or by any electronic, mechanical, or other means, now known or hereafter invented, including photocopying, recording or by use of any storage or retrieval system, without the express written permission of the publisher, except as permitted legally for fair use and educational purposes.

Printed in the United States of America

Cover and book design by Lori Harley

ISBN-13 978-1461180500

12 11 10 09 08 07   5 4 3

This publication contains the ideas of its author. It is intended to provide interesting and thought provoking concepts. It is sold with the understanding that the author and publisher are not offering medical or psychological services. The reader should consult professional advice before personally adopting the ideas and practices within.

Contents

Foreword by Kenneth Ray Stubbs	VII
Preface	XV
Introduction	1
SUZANNE BLACKBURN [MY STORY]	13
JOSEPH KRAMER, PhD	26
ISA MAGDALENA	40
BETTY DODSON, PhD	60
STEVE HOWARD, PhD	70
GINA OGDEN, PhD	82
NUT TMU-ANKH BUTTERFLY	98
ANNIE SPRINKLE, PhD	112
ALEX JADE	124
JULIE BERGER	138
RUDOLPH BALLENTINE, MD	146
SHERI WINSTON, CNM	162
SINGING DEER	178
COLLIN BROWN	188
BOB HAMPTON	202
BETTY MARTIN, DC	212
EMAYA	228
Conclusion: SO, WHERE DO YOU GO FROM HERE?	239
Glossary	243
Resources	251
Acknowledgments	261
About the Author	263

Foreword

An ancient role is reemerging.

For centuries, oppressive religious dogmas conceiving sexual pleasure and orgasm as only a base, often sinful impulse have dominated the Western cultural landscapes. But the times, they are a-changin'. Especially since the 1960s, increasingly we have been stepping outside of the repressive embargoes on exploring and knowing the fullness of our inherent sensual-erotic-sexual nature.

The "bringers of sexual joy"—this is one of the ways the Jungian psychologist Nancy Qualls-Corbett, PhD, characterizes the sacred prostitutes of ancient cultures.[1] Such "bringers" were priest/esses who taught a primordial wisdom too often forgotten, too often suppressed in contemporary Western culture: the profound wisdom of sexual energy.

Today, a number of women and men are evolving this ancient role anew. Drawing from Hindu and Buddhist Tantra, Chinese Taoist sexual teachings and other ancient traditions, as well as contemporary psychological and somatic approaches, these sexual-wisdom teachers are guiding us into a new/ancient paradigm of Eros, a context where sexual energy is an integral, dynamic catalyst for celebration, healing, and transformation. *Reclaiming Eros* is about these new bringers and their visions. To understand their journey though, we must understand a broader conception of our sexual nature than is commonly expressed.

---

1 *The Sacred Prostitute*, p. 34.

Four Models of Our Sexual Nature

In some traditions, the primary or sole espoused purpose of sex is to procreate: "Go forth and multiply" as your God-commanded duty. Sometimes nationalistic governments implore the populous to have offspring in order to fill the armies and factories. In the procreation model, sexual pleasure is either a side effect or a sin. Sexual desire is channeled into having more progeny.

In some cultures, romantic love is proclaimed from the highest hills. The troubadour, the poet, the painter, the playwright, they all glorify the ecstasy of love: "I have often walked down this street before, but the pavement always stayed beneath my feet before." "Everything that touches you touches me." "All you need is love." Genital, sexual pleasure is usually a part of the picture, but the natural high of being in romantic love, relationship, and companionship is portrayed as the supreme expression of sexual attraction.

Sexual pleasure is a third model of human sexual nature. How to be a better, sexier lover is the ubiquitous topic on many newsstand magazine covers. Commercial advertising thrives on sexual imagination, while TV and movie theaters extol Eros. Prostitution is commonly considered one of the world's oldest professions, fulfilling sexual fantasies and desires, while the adult porn and entertainment industry makes billions of dollars providing objects, images, and events that a sizable portion of the population consider sexually pleasurable.

In addition, sex therapy focuses primarily on ways to eliminate sexual dysfunctions that are impediments to experiencing sexual pleasure. Erectile difficulties, inorgasmia, painful intercourse, and lack of sexual desire are common reasons people go to sex therapy; the enormous popularity of the little blue Viagra pill resulted from its efficacy in penile erectility. Whether it is porn, sex therapy, or a horny spring-break encounter in Cancun, it is all in the avowed pursuit of sexual pleasure.

To truly comprehend the lives and visions of the contemporary bringers of sexual joy in this book, however, we must understand a fourth model of our sexual nature. I call it *transformative sexuality*. Other names we could use include sacred or spiritual sexuality, ceremonial sexuality, tantric sexuality, energetic or alchemical sexuality, shamanic sexuality, and transcendent sexuality.

In the *namaste* greeting, we slightly bow with palms together in an expression of prayer to silently acknowledge "the divinity within me embraces the divinity within you." Similarly, in transformative sex, the focus is beyond just being in love with another, beyond birthing offspring, and beyond physical gratification only. We also acknowledge the divinity within the other, which inherently is one with all of divinity. Transformative sex thus becomes a way to dance not only in physical union with another, but to dance in energetic union with the All-That-Is.

To be fully in Oneness with another, with God/Source/Goddess, and with the divinity of all of existence, we must be "born again" with energetic capacities and abilities to "touch" not only the physical, but also the mystical, that which we cannot see or hear with our physical eyes and ears. We must literally trans-form ourselves to intentionally function as more than just a physical body. The primary purpose of the ancient and contemporary sexual-wisdom teacher is to facilitate this transformative development. Various expressions of sexuality and orgasm serve the purpose of birthing this energetic, mystical potential.

Given the sexual repressions/suppressions so many of us carry within, a sexual-wisdom teacher must often begin with fundamental healing approaches just to get us to a point of being able to celebrate our sensual-erotic-sexual self with a genuine aliveness. Then we can really step onto a transformative path that can take us to enlightenment, to being one with God/Source/Goddess, or however we wish to conceptualize our fullest potential.

Such a transformative philosophy is in direct opposition with the currently predominant religious paradigm that holds sex as a major obstacle to developing spiritually and living a righteous life. Yet, in many ancient, so-called "fertility" religions, sexuality was far from being an obstacle. Sexuality was an essential part of communing with the "Sacred Ones." To celebrate ceremonially in physical sexual union was also to celebrate the deities and all of divinity.

To understand the ancient priest/esses' religious functions as "sacred prostitutes" and "sacred whores," we need to realize that their transformative tools were not simply limited to genital sex, and often may not have included any genital sex at all. While in many ways, any consensual sexual act has transformative effects, a profound transformative path engages many aspects of an individual with many different approaches and methods.

In the modern-day West, the conditions, contexts, and culture are radically different from ten thousand or even one thousand years ago. To empower others with primordial sexual-wisdom, the contemporary bringers might utilize any of the following four general modalities.

Four Transformative Modalities

Verbal and visual communication, what I call the *symbolic* modalities, can be very informative and inspiring. Sex education and sex therapy rely primarily on these methods. However, for a bringer of sexual joy to reach the depths of transformative possibilities, additional modalities are usually necessary.

Most sexual-wisdom teachers use *somatic* modalities extensively for such transformative development. Here, the teacher/practitioner might make direct bodily contact. Massage, acupuncture, and chiropractic are standard approaches. A bathing ceremony is a common event, sometimes with feeding. For some, coitus or other forms of erogenous zone stimulation are effective methods. A somatic approach often includes non-contact methods as well, such as chanting, breathing, and yogic stretching practices for opening up restricted energy flows.

A third category of transformative approaches are what I call *emotive* modalities. Here one goes into intense, catalytic states. Deep-trance dance, primal scream, pounding on pillows, and intense breathing patterns are examples. Sometimes the objective is mainly to slip past the analytical, rational, mental processes in order to allow the suppressed parts of ourselves to be experienced and expressed. At other times, the main objective could be to go into ecstatic orgasmic states, perhaps to generate more energy and more pleasure. Another objective could be primarily to go deeply into an altered state to access other dimensions, perhaps to be one with the "Holy Spirit." In a Pentecostal church service, for example, with the organ and piano pounding a primordial beat, the choir clapping and singing while the preacher and congregation are responding in rhythmic exchange, somebody is going to "get happy." In many cases, this "getting happy" by "catching the Holy Spirit" is probably an energetic orgasm, often with the person collapsing to the floor in an ecstatic state, arms and legs flailing in all directions.

Some of the great diversity of BDSM (bondage and discipline, and sadomasochism) practices could be considered as emotive. An observer on the sidelines might consider something humiliating or painful while for the direct recipient of the activities, the words "intense" and "cathartic" might more accurately describe the experience.

A fourth transformative modality is perhaps the most important key to understanding the profound meaningfulness of both the ancient and the contemporary bringer of sexual joy. I term this modality *energetic*. Here, the subtle energies of the bringer literally merge with the student or client. Regardless of whether the bringer is physically touching or not, many have the ability to "touch" energetically. It is possible, for example, to sit several feet away from another and to send energy in a way that results in both having a type of energetic orgasm. This can be done solely with intent, without any intense breathing practice, without any sexy actions, and without any physical stimulation of the body.

Such energetic actions, while often outside of conventional understandings, nonetheless are common with many advanced sexual-wisdom teachers. Sometimes these practitioners, however, do not realize they have developed such "shamanic" abilities; they and their clients/students only know that something "magical" happens, and they seek more of that juice, which is more profound than typical sexual desire and arousal. This is one of the main reasons why the bringers have been so highly regarded in many cultures.

The Bringers

In the ancient cultures that embraced the awesome wisdom and power of sexual energy, the bringers of sexual joy probably used all four of these transformative modalities to various extents with individuals, couples, groups, and the collective culture. These ancient priest/esses no doubt served as teachers, healers, and ceremonialists in all four models of our sexual nature: the procreative, romantic, and pleasurable, in addition to the transformative.

Contemporary bringers, likewise, might utilize any of the four transformative modalities, though their ceremonies and techniques are likely to have evolved specifically for modern-day cultural contexts. Also due to cultural differences, the contemporary bringers seem to focus primarily on the sexual pleasure and transformative models, leaving the procreative and romantic functions to others.

Today the "sacred prostitute" and "sacred whore" terms have become predominant labels in much of the writing on this ancient role while the actual teachers/practitioners usually have elected to refer to themselves as tantrics/tantrikas, dakas/dakinis, sacred intimates, sex coaches, sex surrogates, Quodoushka teachers, priest/esses, sexological bodyworkers, sexual healers, sexual shamans, Tantra teachers, and more. And this list of titles for sexual-energy professionals is growing.

Regardless of which labels the writings or the contemporary bringers use, their functions can be truly understood only within the context of transformation. Sexual wisdom goes far beyond simply fulfilling sexual fantasies. This intrinsic wisdom, instead, expresses itself through a wide spectrum of rhythms in the sexual-energy dance.

Reclaiming Eros presents to us the rhythms of some of the contemporary women and men who have discovered this ancient role reemerging within themselves. They are pioneering a profound new/ancient paradigm that embraces the Oneness of the sexual and the sacred.

As we read their stories, we may find reflections of ourselves. We may find ourselves stepping into this new/ancient paradigm. This is a paradigm of freedom, a paradigm where we can discover our God/Buddha-nature at the core of our Eros.

I sense this reemerging role has profound potential in our modern-day culture. These pioneers are offering us the wisdom they are unfolding. This is a special time. Let's celebrate it!

~ Kenneth Ray Stubbs, PhD

Editor, Contributor, and Publisher:
Women of the Light: The New Sacred Prostitute

Producer and Co-writer:
The Sacred Prostitute documentary

Preface

Three years after the release of the first edition of *Reclaiming Eros*, I have the opportunity to offer a revised second edition. My original intention in writing this book was to share what I had learned about the power of erotic energy. I hoped that sharing these stories would help others claim their own erotic birthright. I'm gratified that so many people have shared with me how the book has touched them in very powerful ways and I hope that this revised edition will continue to have a positive effect on its readers.

To bring new energy to this edition, I have deleted three and added five new chapters. I'm very grateful to be able to include the stories of Gina Ogden, PhD; Betty Martin, DC; and Sheri Winston, CNM. The depth of experience and wisdom these women offer is a gift. They bring fresh insight to the rainbow of perspectives on Eros. I've also added Bob Hampton's story. I'm grateful that Bob was willing to share his experience of the joy that working with a sacred intimate has brought to his life.

The stories herein were created from my interviews with each person. It was tempting to publish the material in interview form, but my first proofread through made it clear that stories distilled and created out of our conversations would be far more engaging. It became my responsibility to convey not only the ideas, but the particular voice and language of each subject through the creation of mini biographies.

As this project evolved, two undeniable truths became clear to me. The first is that the people I have interviewed and written about are alive, highly dynamic, ever-growing and ever-transforming. The second truth is that both the writing of the first book and the revising of this second edition have taken far longer than I ever imagined. Therefore, I must acknowledge that these stories are "told in time" and that the interviewees may have since changed their focus, language and approach. What hasn't changed is the essence of erotic energy and the truth of the messages shared here.

For my own story, I considered writing an entirely new, updated version because I am not the same person that I was in 2007 when the book was first published. They say that you can't step into the same river twice. I think this also true for autobiographical writing. Once you have written your own story, you, the subject, are forever changed. The writing changes you and putting your story out for public viewing really changes you. Ultimately, I choose to let the story stand because it is the transformative lesson of that time and that story that I want to share. The story hasn't really changed even though I have.

Finally, whether you agree or disagree with the words that follow, it is my hope that this book will challenge you to think about Eros and what it means in your life. It is my deepest hope that this work will instigate, provoke, stimulate and inspire expansion.

> *Sex — never repress it! Never be against it.*
> *Rather go deep into it with great clarity, with great love.*
> *Go like an explorer. Sex is just the beginning, not the end.*
> *But if you miss the beginning, you will miss the end also.*
> ~ Osho

Introduction

It was one of those life-defining, pivotal moments — an epiphany. I was lying on the floor, cushioned by a thin foam mat. I was surrounded by about twenty other men and women. We were breathing — just breathing. And even though we were all clothed, it was the most erotically profound moment of my life! Skillfully coached by two teachers, we were using breath to build aliveness in our bodies. After nearly forty-five minutes of intense breathing, the room was wildly alive; emotions unleashed, uninhibited sounds and bodies rocking with feeling. Suddenly, I felt my life force come rushing into my body. I saw it. It looked like the genie coming back into the bottle. My body exploded with life, with erotic charge, with Eros. I was flooded in the most ecstatic way. In the recesses of my being, I remembered that feeling. It was distantly familiar. I had it once, a long time ago. Once had — lost and forgotten — here it was again. I had forgotten what it felt like to be on fire with life. Now I knew again and I cried. Now I would take it back. I would reclaim

Eros—reclaim my life force.

As the room quieted another feeling filled me—gratitude. With tears in my eyes, I looked at the teachers who had guided us through the breathing. I thought, "I'm not sure what angels look like, but I think they might look like that." Who were they? On that day they were teachers, facilitators. On other days they are sacred prostitutes, sacred intimates or sacred whores.

This is a collection of stories about our erotic energy and those who understand it best: today's sacred prostitutes, sacred intimates and teachers. Throughout the course of this writing, the terms "sacred prostitutes," "sacred whores" and "sacred intimates" are used interchangeably, and include those who help others access their own erotic energy for the purposes of healing, regeneration, enlightenment, and sometimes, pure pleasure.

I can hear the questions now, "How dare you use words such as 'whore' or 'prostitute' and 'sacred' together?!" "What can be sacred about prostitution? For that matter, what's sacred about sexuality?" Answering that question is what this book attempts to do. If today's cultural norms are to be accepted, then nothing is sacred about sex and absolutely nothing is sacred about prostitutes. But to work with erotic energy in a way that honors and calls forth the divinity in all of us is sacred. To the sacred prostitute, everything about sexuality is sacred, and our bodies are the direct expression of our divine creation. The erotic energy that we feel in our bodies is the ever-present life force in everything. It is life itself.

After centuries of sexual repression and slander, the world would have us believe that sex is the least sacred of all human interests, and that those who dare to delve deeply into the world of sex are the most profane of all beings. Over 1600 years ago, St. Augustine pronounced the doctrine that "'concupiscence' is the root of original sin and the means of transmitting Adam's guilt to all generations."[1] The Christian church ran with this thought, though not without allies in many of the world's religious systems, and must be credited with executing an impressively effective smear campaign against sexuality.

The waves of damage this campaign has generated are incalculable. Therapists agree that there is a clear connection between sexual repression and the development of damaging and dangerous sexual behaviors, sexual obsessions, dysfunctional relationships, violence, depression, physical disease and more. Rudy Ballentine and Steve Howard (their stories are found in the following pages) both discuss these concepts from the perspective of mental health professionals who have overcome much of their own previous conditioning and worked with others struggling to do so. It's a strenuous mental exercise to imagine how different our lives might be if we lived in a world that celebrated our sexuality, rather than condemning it as inherently evil.

According to Webster's, a whore is "a woman who engages in illegal sexual intercourse, especially one who engages in promiscuous sexual intercourse for pay; a prostitute; a harlot."[2] Though this is the currently accepted definition, the original meanings were quite

---

1 Walker, *The Women's Encyclopedia of Myths and Secrets*, p. 911. San Francisco: Harper Collins, 1983.

2 *Webster's New Twentieth Century Dictionary, 2nd edition*, p. 1446. Boston: Prentice Hall Press, 1979.

different. In fact, the word "whore" comes from quite a noble source. Egyptian temple priestesses were called Ladies of the Hour. Each was entrusted with the protection of the solar boat of the sun god Ra as he passed through her hour of darkness, making his way across the underworld. Thus, the Dance of the Hours celebrates the divine whores, the Horea, who were the keepers of the night hours. In Persia, the Ladies of the Hour were called Houris; in Babylon, Harine; and among the Semites, Hor. The Horea tended the souls of those in their care, guarded the gates of heaven, and trained men in the sexual mysteries. The oldest Hebrew folk dance, the Hora, is named after the circle dances of the sacred harlots.

Other cultures celebrated sexuality as a spiritual force as well. The Devadasi, the prostitute-priestesses of the Hindu Temples, and the Vestal Virgins of ancient Rome, were among the women (and men) from many cultures that were regarded as the embodiment of Goddess (or God). By merging with those temple priestesses or prostitutes in holy ceremonial union, devotees became united with the divine.[3] In ancient Egypt, the temple prostitutes were known to be healers. Their very fluids were said to have the power to cure. In Greece, the temples of Aphrodite were served by thousands of sacred harlots, and when the wives of Hellenic Greece were reduced to the status of servants, courtesans remained politically and legally equal to men.[4]

Like the ancients, today's sacred prostitutes serve a higher power

---

3 Qualls–Corbett, Nancy. *The Sacred Prostitute: Eternal Aspect of the Feminine*, p. 68. Toronto: Inner City Books, 1988.

4 Walker. *The Women's Encyclopedia*, pp. 819-826.

by honoring the whole human being, recognizing the indivisibility of sex and spirit. These women and men embody Goddess and God, using the power of Eros to raise consciousness, to lift spirits, and to heal. Today's sacred prostitutes know that we all possess an embodied wisdom and creative power that can be accessed through Eros. They know that erotic expression is divine expression, and that lovemaking is a sacred act. They know that life can be lived more fully when wholeness is achieved, and they know that wholeness happens when we embrace all parts of ourselves, including our erotic, sexual selves.

Erotic energy is the pulse, the animation, the life energy, the ever-present essential force in everything—everything, including, but not exclusively, our genitals. This powerful force cannot be denied. It is relentless. It will, against all resistance, persist, because the vitality of life depends on it. Erotic energy can be mutated and suppressed. It can be turned inside out, so that its expression is pornographic, corrupt or even violent, but it cannot be destroyed.

It is often through erotic energy (not exclusively experienced in connection with another person), that we experience our connection with the divine, our connection to the One, our Oneness. It is when we bring our bodies together in erotic union or in direct connection with divinity that we are most in harmony with all of creation. To be human is to be erotic. To be erotic is to be alive.

This concept of sacred sexuality was new to me. Like most people, I grew up with the teaching that sex was solely for heterosexual married couples. Married monogamy was the only acceptable arrangement, and even that was too base for polite conversation.

Talking about sex openly would ruin one's "good reputation." Even thinking about sex too much or in the "wrong way" probably meant there was something very wrong with you. Anyone who exchanged money for sex was, at best, pathetic.

When I heard the word "whore" or "prostitute," I imagined a mildly attractive, weary woman who stepped out into the dark night to begin her sordid work. She strolled up and down the street in spiked heels, rolling her hips inside her too-tight, too-short skirt. Her overly ample make-up advertised like a neon sign. She was a woman of low morality and low self-esteem. She'd sell sex to anyone willing to pay. She might be an addict. She was certainly a damaged woman with a shameful past. She was foul and corrupt.

Or I might have created another image. This one was of a woman who didn't do her marketing on the street. This woman took referrals and made appointments with her clients. She was beautiful, smart and socially skillful. An evening with her might start with dinner at a nice restaurant. Later, keeping her feelings aloof, she would artfully treat her client to extraordinary sex in exchange for a lot of money. Occasionally, I would imagine a good looking young man who went to auditions by day and cleverly turned "tricks" for older gentlemen by night.

These are just some of the stereotypical images I had of prostitutes, and there are some who live such lives. However, I now have other images as well, which include Tantra teachers, group facilitators, theater artists, doctors, psychotherapists, modern sacred prostitutes and sacred intimates who happily chose their vocations. Unlike their ancient counterparts, today's sacred whores do not have a community temple in which they work. They are creating their own temples, designing their own rituals, and creating their own history. They are following a call of spirit that transcends time and space. They follow this call against all modern acceptance and social support.

I've come to a new understanding of and reverence for sacred prostitutes, sacred whores and sacred intimates. Because of the gifts they have given me, I want to tell some of the stories of the courageous, powerful, and critically important work they do. This is only a sampling and does not tell the whole story. There are many more people engaged in this work. Each of them has special gifts and unique stories to share.

The women and men I interviewed for this book have an amazing range of talents and education. They hold master's degrees in social work, doctorates in psychology, psychiatry and human sexuality. Some fight for political justice, some are parents, some are active in their churches, some work in public health, and some are happily married. Each one of them contributes her or his own unique life experiences to their work. What is consistent among them is that all are dedicated to living with the joy of vibrant sexuality, and in the ecstasy of being connected to all of creation.

One of the impressive qualities I noticed in everyone interviewed for this book was that of unfettered hospitality. That is, every individual expressed complete welcoming, complete acceptance, of those who came to them. This alone is life affirming and healing. Everyone I interviewed is committed to lovingly guiding others as they seek to recover from shame, explore new aspects of erotic energy, and learn to love and embrace divinity in themselves and in others.

Here, also, are four clients' stories: Steve Howard's, Julie Berger's, Bob Hampton's, and mine. There are many reasons why someone might seek a sacred intimate's services or attend a workshop that focuses on erotic energy. Some people go because they need to be touched in a way that includes and honors all of their being. Some go because they have been deeply wounded, and seek out deep healing. Some go because they want to know more about their bodies; they want education. Some go because they find the kind of caring, presence, and acceptance they long for and can find nowhere else. Often people may not even know why they go. They may simply be compelled by some powerful force to seek out a way to be fully alive. They dare to claim a life of vitality, joy, affirmation and wholeness. To pursue such a life is an act of courage.

During the writing of this book, two questions arose over and over. Why is it important to recognize the sacredness of our eroticism? How does erotic energy work? In some ways, attempting to find answers only leads to more questions. The task is not unlike answering how prayer works or why babies thrive when they are held. It just does, and they just do. Still, this is the age of science, and we are curious creatures wanting to know what makes us tick. So, to the best of my ability, I am attempting to shed some light on these questions if not fully answer them.

Each person interviewed for this book has developed great understanding of erotic power. Some have spent a lifetime teasing out a better understanding and ability to articulate the "science" of Eros. Isa Magdalena, Collin Brown, Emaya, Alex Jade and others, through much experience, have begun to understand and explain erotic energy in a comprehensive way. Psychologist Steve Howard and psychiatrist Rudy Ballentine offer insights on internalized shame, the burden of that shame, and what embracing our natural eroticism can do to relieve that burden. Betty Dodson, Joseph Kramer, Gina Ogden and Annie Sprinkle must be acknowledged as true pioneers in the effort to reclaim the essence of our nature. It is my hope that all of these stories will further increase understanding among those who read them.

I have done my best to retell these stories accurately. When the character or flavor of the interview was contrary to proper grammar or sentence structure, I have favored the flavor. (I am more committed to conveying the essence of these individuals than I am to making my grammar teachers proud.) When stream-of-consciousness conversation challenged understandable reading I favored the reading. Where the flow of the interview was erratic or out of sequence, changes have been made to convey the story in an understandable fashion. Every person interviewed shared his or her own unique experiences and perspectives on this subject. The beliefs expressed in each story are those of the original storyteller.

I am compelled to tell the story of sacred whores and sacred intimates because my life has been so powerfully transformed by some of these men and women and the experiences they have guided me through. Some of these people have been my teachers. Many of them are now my friends. My life is infinitely more joyful because of all of them. Still, this isn't an easy story for me to tell. This subject makes a lot of people, including myself, uncomfortable. Telling this story feels risky. I'm sure I will alienate some and offend others. But it is my hope that this book will shine a light on the extraordinary power of erotic energy to heal, to make whole and to bring joy.

During my interview with Betty Dodson, I told her that I was having trouble writing. I told her I was holding back because of the risk of exposing myself. Betty, who clearly knows what happens when you expose yourself, told me, "Telling the truth takes guts! Going all the way may be further than you want to go. That's the first thing you've got to confront. If you can't go all the way, don't go at all!" Since I know that Betty is right, and because other brave friends have urged me to write fearlessly, I have included my own story in this book.

It is important to understand how terms are being used in the pages that follow. I have included a glossary as a reference for terms used throughout this book. But I want to be clear, from the start, that "Eros" or "erotic energy" refers to far more than genital feelings — more than what most people understand as sex. Eros is libidinal, life-affirming energy. Taoism refers to it as *ching chi* or life source. When I use the words sex, sexual and sexwork, it is with a broad brush meant to include many different experiences and styles of working with erotic energy.

Most of the people in this book do not have sex with their clients in any commonly understood sense of the term. They are sacred erotic healers, however, because they have learned to access, manage, and exchange erotic energy while respecting their own boundaries and those of their clients. Terms such as "sexwork," "erotic education," "sacred prostitution" or "sacred intimacy" in this context mean sharing erotic energy with another and with the divine. It is also important to acknowledge that some of the individuals whose stories are included here do not identify as sacred intimates or prostitutes. They may use other terms such as teacher, guide, healer, priest or priestess to describe themselves. I have chosen to use these identifiers in an effort to reclaim the honor they were once given.

The word "healer" is a term of convenience saving us much paraphrasing. The people and the work described in the following pages facilitate or midwife transformation; they create a container and set a stage where healing can happen. I do not believe that one person actually heals another. We each carry our own seeds, our own potential to heal and be whole. Healing comes from within when conditions allow.

We live in a world that desperately needs healing. We need to wake up to the damage we have suffered from sexual repression. The ravages of denying what is core to our humanity show up on our front pages daily. "We could not do the things we do to ourselves, to each other or to the planet if we truly felt connected," Singing Deer tells us. On the other hand, pleasure induces feelings of well-being, connection, states of splendid innocence and delight. Great harmony blossoms when we allow ourselves to enjoy pleasure — to be fully erotic beings, capable of loving ourselves, loving others, and feeling the totality of our connection to all.

*All sorrows can be borne
if we put them in a story or tell a story about them.*
~ Isak Dinesen, *Out of Africa*

Suzanne Blackburn
[my story]

Much of my story is cruelly common, and that is the most compelling reason to tell it. Part of my story is particularly uncommon; another compelling reason. My life, like any life, is a tapestry of stories within a story, and I know now that I am the author of these stories, creating them through the decisions that I've made along the way. For a very long time most of my life stories were deeply influenced by three monsters: shame, fear and confusion. These unconscious but relentless forces stood behind most of the decisions I've made and the life lens I've looked through. The prevailing theme of my story is how I ran away from myself to escape the three monsters. I ran away from my feelings and hid behind a heavy steel door marked "I don't feel." I have been trying to come back through that same door ever since.

The beginning is simple. I was sexually violated sometime around the age of four. I wish I could describe how hard it has been to accept that this could actually happen to me. Though some details are fuzzy, what I do know is that the events were terrifying and that they left me with a sense of mistrust and doubt about my lovability that has permeated every aspect of my life. I was hurt by one person and abandoned by another. They were supposed to protect me. My world turned inside out. I learned to mistrust everyone and everything. I especially mistrusted my own worth. I lost any real sense of personal power or place in the world, and I was filled with overwhelming shame—too much shame to speak of—so I kept silent and pretended to be okay, extra-okay in fact. I presented so well that nobody could see what was really inside of me. It felt like a safe way to move through the world.

I was betrayed again at the ages of sixteen and seventeen. On two separate occasions, by two separate men, I was raped. I didn't walk into dark alleys or bad neighborhoods, nor did I encounter deranged or outwardly violent social outcasts. I didn't have to. I was raped by one man who was my supervisor at a summer camp, and by a "nice" young man on a blind date. By this point in my life, I owned my shame so well that I blamed myself, and I conspired with my violators by holding both violent events secret for another twenty-nine years. I kept our nasty little secret buried with my pain under many lonely layers while I compulsively replayed the events in my head—as if by doing so, I could somehow change the outcome. I couldn't. Instead I became the perpetrator as well as the victim as I continued to abuse myself by replaying that horrible, inescapable loop, remembering and reliving the events over and over.

Powerless to change the past, I developed an exhausting, chronic posture of hyper-vigilance, protecting myself from the "next time."

My body was always in the tension of fight or flight. Having someone stand or walk behind me made me squirm. I feared going to bed. Most nights my sleep was disrupted with panic. The worst, most costly aftershock was disassociation, which allowed me to avoid any feelings other than anger. I was capable of being totally immersed in an event, apparently involved with other people, aware of the associated feelings, but experiencing nothing. I recognized the feelings in my mind, but had no visceral experience of them. Movies became very important to me. Movies took me outside myself and into the characters' experiences. What happened on the screen was safely separate from me. A deep part of me was hungry to feel alive, so movies gave me a safe way to feel.

My favorite children's story was (and still is) *Pinocchio*. I could really relate to the little wooden guy. Just like Pinocchio, I longed to be real and feel alive. Like him I just wanted to be real. I wanted to be seen and accepted, but I was afraid, so I tried very hard to be someone else. Part of me longed to be accepted, yet much of me begged to be hidden away.

My solution was to create two separate people: one to hide and one to show. One of these people I kept locked inside like some crazy old aunt who embarrassed me. She was my shameful little secret. I denied her existence to the world. The other person was the one I allowed the world to see the one I wanted to be. I created her, making her a strong and colorful character. I made her big enough to draw attention from the crazy aunt, and I practiced this charade so long that it seemed normal to me. I often forgot about the crazy aunt in the attic and believed entirely in the sole existence of my character.

Underneath my presentation, I was chronically unhappy, lonely, and exhausted, but I didn't know a better way to live. Most importantly, I didn't realize the cost. I didn't realize that I was spending enormous amounts of energy hiding, pretending, and struggling just to appear okay. I didn't realize how much of my life I was missing in this disassociated state. I watched my life go by on a screen, and I missed the full experience of it. This shouldn't have happened. It shouldn't happen to anyone! It is theft—theft of life.

Like Pinocchio, I was rescued by the miracle of love and brought back to life. For me, this miracle came when I became a mom. When my first daughter was born, a powerful force broke through the wall I had built around myself. I believe that the passion of maternal love was great enough to pry me open, and once the barriers were breached, many feelings, some beautiful beyond words, some not so sweet, began to flow. Sweet or not, the good news was that I began to feel.

Some of what I began to feel manifested in a twenty-year battle with serious insomnia. In the very early morning hours I would awaken in panic. With my heart racing, it would be hours before I could eat, drink, medicate or otherwise numb myself back to sleep. During those sleepless hours, I developed a world of rich, dark fantasies to distract and sooth myself. (I also developed addictions to food and alcohol.) As I look back, I find it hard to understand why I let myself go through almost every night in such turmoil or how I found enough energy to push through each day. I wonder why I didn't see what a deadly pattern this was or why I didn't ask for help sooner. I've heard that if you drop a frog into boiling water, the frog will immediately try to jump to safety. However, if you put a frog into warm water and slowly bring the water to a boil, the frog will not jump out. My pot came to a boil very slowly. I didn't jump.

It was only will and the love that I felt for my daughters that carried me through my life. I had no real "juice," no passion and little life force. It was only a matter of time before my strength of will ran out and exhaustion rescued me. Yes, rescued me. I think it just hit me one day—something was very, very wrong with my life. I was drained, empty and scared, and I had to learn to live differently. When I finally realized how much hot water I was in, I was near collapse. I desperately needed help, but I didn't know where or how to ask for it. I had no experience of being cared for or supported, but some inner survivor came forward to help me make changes—big changes! I divorced my husband of twenty-three years, left my business, moved to a new home with my daughters, started a new business, and began to search for a way of being more alive. For the first time, I realized that I needed something big in my life—something much bigger than myself. I sought out various spiritual paths, experimented with Holotropic Breathwork, joined a meditation circle and started seeing a psychotherapist. I got a glimpse of what really being alive felt like. It felt good, and I was hungry for more. I wanted to explore everything.

Curiosity (and maybe some other powerful forces) led me to a Body Electric workshop for men and women in the fall of 2000. To say that this radical workshop challenged and changed me would be a gross understatement. I found myself in a world of experiences unlike anything I could have even imagined! In an environment that felt wonderfully safe and supportive, we were taught to use breathing to move out of our minds and into our bodies. We danced to express what it was like for each of us to be in our unique bodies. We honored each other with ritual undressing and sensual massage. Then we were guided through giving and receiving erotic massages with reverence. The first time I ever consciously experienced a sense of wholeness was in that workshop. I began to see the divine innocence of my body and my feelings as I experienced a long-awaited, joyful homecoming. I began to feel more at ease and more alive within. I became aware of a core shift as shame began to drop away to make room for self-acceptance. Disassociation began to dissolve into wholeness and loneliness began to surrender to spiritual communion. My experiences there initiated a process of change and set me on a spiritual path of reclaiming myself.

That weekend I soaked up many rich ideas and new concepts. During one lunch break, I overheard someone ask, "What is a sacred intimate?" I was instantly intrigued, so I paid close attention to the answer. "Well, as a sacred intimate, I work to help people increase their flow of erotic energy and to see themselves as sacred beings. We are erotic by nature, and I recognize that everything, including pleasure, is sacred. What I actually do depends on the person I am working with, their needs and desires. I might offer an erotic massage or give someone a delicious, sensuous bath or just hold someone closely and tenderly. I might just listen. Sometimes people just want to be heard. I might be asked to teach a client about his or her body. I try to address each person's needs and find a way to answer them that is within my own boundaries. Whatever the scenario, I try to accept each person lovingly and without judgment. It's more about how, than what, I do."

Okay, I thought, that's a slightly vague but very intriguing answer. During the next two years, I learned much more about sacred intimacy, experiencing firsthand the healing that can happen when we learn to accept love and celebrate ourselves. With each experience, I grew more comfortable, more delighted and more alive. Within the embrace of erotic community, I faced and shed layers of my past. After a lifetime of living outside of my body and having little sense of worthiness and no sense of sacredness, I began to reclaim myself, my body and my erotic life, and found an unimagined richness there. That richness transferred to other areas of my life — in fact, all areas. I felt more alive in every part of my life.

I became very interested in how sacred intimates work with erotic energy. I wanted to know more about this uncommon capacity to love and the healing power of erotic energy. I flirted with the idea of using erotic touch in my own bodywork practice, so I signed up for the sacred intimate training that The Body Electric School offered. The training was intense. I dubbed it "erotic boot camp." More than twenty men and women spent six days living, talking, breathing, laughing, crying, embracing, pleasuring, witnessing and loving each other as we learned how to work with clients as sacred intimates or sacred prostitutes. This workshop brought an exciting mix of people together. Some of the participants were full-service prostitutes. Some were massage therapists. There were teachers, doctors, sex coaches and artists. Some participants were there to develop their current sacred intimate practices. Some were just curious and wanted to explore sexuality on a deeper personal plane. Most, like me, were powerfully drawn to the work because of the healing they'd experienced in their own process.

During the training, I witnessed and experienced more of the amazing healing that happens in the presence of powerful erotic experiences. I reaffirmed that Eros is vital to our well-being. Free-flowing erotic energy is as vital as wholesome food and clean water. I learned these things and I felt more alive than I could remember ever feeling. But still I was a product of my culture—a sexually repressive culture. Deeply embedded in me was a value system with a very narrow range of what is acceptable, causing me to wrestle countless rounds with my own value system. I wrestled with the difficult question of how honest I dared to be about my beliefs and my personal experiences. In the company of like-minded people, I dared. I was open and enthusiastic about my feelings and convictions. Elsewhere, I kept an important part of my life experience hidden. I was afraid of being criticized and shamed for expressing these countercultural beliefs. Again, I became a different person inside than the one I presented to the world. I had been here before and this time I knew, too well, the cost of living with such a split.

My internal battles are not over. I am still caught in the crossfire of my experience and my culturally instilled and reinforced beliefs. This continues to be a difficult process for me, and I feel my resistance and fear strengthening as I write this story. No matter how strong the inner conflict, I feel that I have to try to tell my story honestly. What I've experienced over the past few years has changed me in a radical way. The transformation is more than a knowing or a belief. It's a primal truth. It's as much a part of me as my skin or my blood. It's hard, even impossible, to describe. I only know for certain that something very important has changed, and so I am doing my best to articulate it.

One experience that stands out happened in a session with a sacred intimate who I will call Aaron. I was feeling particularly unhappy and angry with myself about how I so often betrayed my own boundaries to give in to another's desire. Repeatedly, I kept my own needs or limits hidden so that I could avoid disappointing someone else. I knew that I did this for fear of losing another's love or approval. This was an old story of mine. I knew that I wanted to change the story, but I felt powerless. I went to Aaron realizing that he didn't have a magic formula, but I hoped he could offer me some help. I told him about my struggle with this old story and how these feelings had been triggered by a recent incident at a party. I felt that I had handled the moment badly. I was frustrated. I was afraid I'd never be able to be clear and strong about my needs and my limits, and I was ashamed.

Aaron asked a few questions, and when we both felt clear about our intentions, he suggested that we begin with some bodywork. He asked me to keep my focus on my fear and frustration. By that time, I only wanted to escape into the pleasure of a good massage. I just wanted to bury my feelings, but he encouraged me to stay present. He coached me to deepen my breath to allow as much feeling as possible to come into my awareness. Aaron explained that it was in this way that a real internal shift might happen. We talked about what would happen during the bodywork session. We agreed on the boundaries.

We began by taking a few deep breaths together. Aaron helped me undress. I wanted to trust him. As I lay on his massage table, he adjusted the top sheet to keep me warm. His hands felt delightfully warm. I felt myself begin to unwind, relax, and let go of the anger, the frustration, and the chaos that was swirling in my head. I lost track of my focus and I lost track of time as I allowed my body to drink in the deliciousness of his touch. He prompted me to continue to take deep, full breaths. He massaged my entire body, and soon I was riding an intense, ecstatic wave. Aaron helped me stay on the wave, coaching me how to use my breath and PC muscle contractions. It was extraordinary.

Suddenly, Aaron leaned into the table, pushed his hips against my side and said, "You want more, don't you?" He started breathing heavily. My mind, temporarily off-line, reconnected as I mentally scrambled for a response. In an instant, a crowd of thoughts assembled in my head, "What does he mean? We set the boundaries! I trusted him! We had an agreement. What does he want? What do I want?" Why was he breaking the boundaries we agreed on? There it was again. There was my old struggle to know what I wanted, to feel powerful and strong. I realized that Aaron had deliberately set me up for this challenge to help me find my power. Even though I knew he was role-playing, it was very convincing and took me into very real feelings. I just wanted to sink back into the yummy touch. I didn't want to struggle, but I had come here to make a change in my life. So I said, "No," and used my hand to push him back a bit.

He insisted again, and again I said, "No."

Aaron continued the massage and left the words behind. I was really flying. Suddenly he pushed up against me again. What was he doing? I was frustrated, confused and annoyed, but I didn't want to offend him or make him angry! I didn't want to drive him away. There it was again. Wasn't I always confused about and afraid to claim what I really wanted? Wasn't I always more concerned with someone else's feelings than with my own? Aaron stopped pressing me, and one more time we fell into merciful silence.

Once again, I let go of all the chatter in my head and allowed the soft touch of his hands to raise the erotic sensation in my body. I don't know how much time passed, but I do know that the charge in my body increased, and soon I was close to cascading into an orgasm—I was right on the edge. Aaron started to pressure me again—his timing was brilliant. At the moment of orgasmic explosion, a huge "NO!" erupted from deep within my belly. With the waves of orgasm washing over me, a flood of struggle left my body. I broke into heavy sobs. Aaron held me; I thought I would never stop crying.

With my eyes still closed, I looked down inside myself as if I could see the inside of my belly. There, I saw a long, thick scar, which I recognized as a scar from the wound of being violated. I had worked so hard to heal that wound, but in that moment I knew the scar would never go away. It was only by recognizing and accepting the scar that I could be free from the legacy of my story and reclaim my power. The vision and the lesson were so much more than just a thought or a belief. It was a deeply embodied experience. A structural change had taken place, and the lesson became fixed in my body. I felt exhausted, but peaceful, sure and centered.

That experience was a critical turning point for me. It was so strong and so clear that I could no longer doubt, minimize or withhold what I knew of the healing power of Eros. After my session with Aaron I decided that I had to write about sacred intimacy. I wanted the world to know that this type of healing was a possibility. I felt a responsibility to share the wonder of what I'd learned.

In the same way that trauma sent me into hiding and kept me from being fully in my life, healing brought me out to join the celebration of living. Healing took me out of a world of shades of gray into the land of vibrant color. My entire world is more colorful, more exciting, more fun, more fulfilling, more everything. Time spent with my family and friends brings me expansive joy. I'm more confident, creative and energetic about my work. I sleep soundly, pleasure is greater, laughter comes easily, and occasionally tears flow without restraint. I feel more connected, more loving and more compassionate. I do not feel alone in my secrecy and shame. I know that I am loved and that I belong in this world. I'm finally a real live woman—very alive.

Pinocchio's story ended happily ever after. Fairy tales are tidy that way—life isn't. My ending hasn't been written yet. I feel that most of my life has been given back to me and I'd love to be able to say that I'm fully healed, that everything is perfect, but that's not quite so. I've awakened the awesome force of Eros within me and changes are happening fast—very fast. The change can be overwhelming at times and difficult to integrate into a world that doesn't hold the erotic as sacred. Occasionally I still wake up in fear, and occasionally

I still feel numb and cut off from my feelings. At these times, I feel frustrated because the healing isn't complete. I write because the writing helps me, and I hope that it will eventually help others. I continue to explore Eros as I continue to work toward wholeness and joy. My path is one of joy and challenge, happiness and pain, and I am grateful for it all.

Joseph Kramer's gentle, thoughtful, articulate manners and boy-next-door looks do much to soften the edges of his very radical work. Working on an instructional video about vulva massage is just another task in Joe's day. He makes it all seem so very normal — and perhaps it is. Joe is the founder of The Body Electric School, a major influence in the reclaiming Eros movement. Joe's current endeavor is The New School of Erotic Touch. I asked Joe if he identified as a tribal elder. With a barley audible groan, he replied "more and more every day." Joseph also identifies as a visionary, teacher, sacred slut and erotic shaman. He is unwavering in his enthusiasm for learning and teaching about human sexuality. "As a visionary, my role is to understand a system, embody the vision, share, and then move on to the next thing." It is impossible to measure the contribution Joe has made toward creating a sex-positive world where people can celebrate their sexuality, be free from shame, and make educated choices about what they do with their bodies. But it's clear that many, many lives, including mine, are far richer and healthier because of his work.

PHOTO CREDIT: DARREN AVILA

Joseph Kramer, PhD

I grew up in a Catholic family that was very service oriented—very "other" conscious. My father was a lawyer who gave half of his time providing free services for the underprivileged and folks in trouble, so early on I got this idea of service and connectedness to others. I was a very religious, and I would say, ecstatic boy. Something my father and grandmother instilled in me was a sense of awe and a love of nature. Even in my suburban neighborhood, I tried to get away and spend time in some little field or wooded area. As I got older,

I channeled that sense of awe and wonder into mystical Christianity.

In the Catholic community, there is often recognition when someone is gay. The mother or father or the whole social structure sees that this is a boy or a girl who is oriented differently. This recognition is written into the Catholic subculture, and that's why there are so many Catholic priests who are gay. There's not an acknowledgment *per se,* and people will not say, "Oh, he's gay." What they do say, what they said to me countless times, from the time I was ten years old was, "Ah, I think you have a vocation. You should be a priest." Nuns and priests told me this. My parents were a little cooler about it, but clearly their vision was for me to be a priest.

At seventeen, straight out of high school, I gave up masturbation and joined the Society of Jesus, a Roman Catholic religious community also known as the Jesuits. For the next ten years I was tutored in the Jesuit path of the ecstatic celibate. It was a mystical, ecstatic path — a path of service. What I got from the Jesuits was the vision "to be a man for others." Along with that, I was made aware of my responsibility to gain skills and education so that I could be in service in the best possible way. I was taught to embody the divine — to be a person for others in the name of the incarnate god, Jesus. They called it, "To become other Christs." Later I would see that this calling is the same as that of the sacred prostitute who embodies the god or goddess they serve.

During my ten-year-long training with the Jesuits, I received one full-body massage. That massage woke up such extraordinary new levels of consciousness in me that I thought, "That was the most important two hours of my life!" I had a new sense of embodiment and a new sense of wholeness as if long-separated pieces of me had been brought back together. At the age of twenty-eight, after giving celibacy a real fair try, I realized that I could no longer deny the world of bodily sensation. I realized I did not have "the gift of celibacy." With great sadness, I came to realize that the Jesuits were not the community for me. I recognized that there were many people who were priests and nuns because they felt called to something and saw only one way, but I knew that for me there was more and wanted to explore my options.

I realized I did not have "the gift of celibacy."

I left the celibate seminary life to explore gay life in New York City. At this time, the late 1970s and early 1980s, AIDS was taking an enormous toll on gay men, and there developed not just fear, but terror about sex. Many men isolated themselves and just stopped having any intimate connection at all. The need for safe, sexual sensation and connection was vital. My Jesuit training—my commitment to serving others—led me to become a masseur. So I left New York for a month long trip to California to study Esalen massage. Though not sexual, the long, sensuous strokes were intensely pleasurable and capable of producing delightful trance states. I found that I had a gift for touch. I did not imagine erotic massage until some time later when several of my clients made, not salacious, but genuine, heartfelt requests for healing sexual touch. Realizing that erotic massage offered the possibility of safe sexual connection, I began to offer this touch as part of my practice.

The erotic massage I developed was actually based on my

experience of oral sex, but because of the risk of HIV/AIDS, the massage couldn't be oral. It had to be touch, and actually, I think that hands offer more expansive stimulation than the mouth and throat. I observed that when erotic energy got activated or awakened in this expansive way, men experienced new power and a new sense of self. I began to think of myself as an erotic shaman.

That was the genesis of Taoist Erotic Massage. I used the term "Taoist," because that was my interpretive system. I had studied acupressure; I knew the meridian system of the body, and I thought, "This is about circulation of erotic energy throughout the body, through the meridians." According to Taoist thought, our genitals are generators of energy. It was possible to learn to circulate the erotic energy, not release it, so that men could sustain high states of arousal and build enormous energy. This is very different from the traditional sex model which I call "balloon sex," where the goal is only to build to a climax. I'm not one who says that men should never ejaculate, but in my teaching, I do say, "You people have doctoral degrees in ejaculation by this time. Why not try non-ejaculation and see what happens?" I feel that it's very important that men know that they have a choice and that they know what the opportunities are.

According to Taoist thought, our genitals are generators of energy.

To enhance the effectiveness of the massage, I taught my clients to breathe using a kind of conscious breathing called Rebirthing Breath, which I learned in a year-long training program with

Claire Arnesen. This breathing process circulates energy, charges the body, and can bring about blissful, full-body states of reality as well as emotional release and transformation. In addition to the training, I scheduled twenty-five individual sessions with Claire. Sitting with me for hours coaching and observing my breathing, Claire recognized the severe, armor-creating shame I had developed growing up a homosexual boy in a conservative Catholic culture. She suggested that I do erotic meditation exercises to relieve my body of the armoring.

During the exercises I was to masturbate, use the Rebirthing Breath and visualize healthy, affirming scenes with important people from my past. I visualized my father regarding me with approval for my sexuality. I visualized my mother loving every part of me—even my homosexuality. I masturbated and breathed while visualizing being in the church; in the school of my youth. I even masturbated with Jesus looking on while he told me of his unconditional love. Claire had me repeat the exercises over and over during a three month period. With every repetition, I became freer, more alive and healthier.

I also borrowed an exercise called the Big Draw from contemporary Taoist master Mantak Chia, and used it to help my clients move into higher levels of feeling. The Big Draw allows people to have full-body, orgasmic experiences without discharging ejaculate or, if you are in the energy model, without discharging the energy. The Big Draw pumps the orgasmic energy from the genitals, up the back, down through the center of the front of the body, and back into the genitals. With erotic massage, rhythmic breathing and the Big Draw in combination, men were having experiences that were ecstatic, prolonged, multi-orgasmic and transformative. They were regularly seeing visions and going into deep trances very much like LSD induced states of consciousness or a state akin to runner's high. Something big was happening.

Over a thousand massages later, I founded The Body Electric School of Massage and Rebirthing with Claire Arnesen onboard to teach the Rebirthing courses. Because I had found other massage classes to be homophobic, I was determined to offer a professional massage certification in a homosexual-friendly environment. That was 1984, and the beginning of The Body Electric School which takes its name from Walt Whitman's poem, "I Sing the Body Electric." I was drawn to Whitman not only because he was a great poet, but because he was gay and because of his years of service nursing the wounded and dying during the Civil War.

Inspired by Whitman and by the HIV/AIDS crisis sweeping the San Francisco Bay area, I hired Irene Smith, a masseuse for people with AIDS. Irene's training in touch for people with life-threatening illnesses became part of the required curriculum. I left erotic massage out of the curriculum while I continued to offer it in private practice. The need for education about safe, erotic touch was clear, but so was my fear of losing my license from the state of California. By 1986, I could no longer allow my fears to keep me from teaching hands-on safe sex in the form of the Taoist Erotic Massage.

I knew I had opened up a very powerful medium with Taoist Erotic Massage, and perhaps because I had seen the power of the community coming together for Catholic Mass, I suspected that the power would be greatly amplified when experienced in group or tribe. Indeed, I found that even though the physiological response to extended erotic sensation was the same during a private session as it was in a group, the outcome proved to be quite different. Experiencing a high level of erotic arousal in a group context had the potential to bring about far more substantial change. I believe it is in the group or tribal setting that we need to shake off shame, because that is where so much shame is put upon us. If in a group context, we're seen as erotic beings and affirmed for it rather than shamed for it, we can better step into what is erotically possible, what is humanly possible; so I began to develop and offer classes. What I did was simply bring people together to explore erotic and ecstatic states. I wanted to have a place where the rules were changed and where we could really get involved in being fully embodied, erotic, whole human beings.

I believe it is in the group or tribal setting that we need to shake off shame, because that is where so much shame is put upon us.

In these groups, I noticed that the men who tried to hang on or keep control had very ordinary experiences. I realized I needed a two-day program with the first day being choreographed exercises designed to help people take down their barriers and build up their trust. By the second day, possessing a greater sense of trust, they could better surrender to the erotic touch and the high states of consciousness it aroused. The more the men surrendered, the higher they went, the more powerful their experience. Surrender is a very important spiritual teaching in most religions, and here it was in a very physical form where the quality of the experience depended not on doing, but on letting go. It is interesting that the Kama Sutra has nine chapters dedicated to oral sex in which men are schooled to be totally receptive; to surrender. Many participants reported life-changing experiences which included letting go of fears and healing of past traumas. Many experienced a feeling of love for the whole world, a feeling of body and spirit coming together. Some reported having a direct experience of God.

Surrender is a very important spiritual teaching in most religions, and here it was in a very physical form.

I believe that the biggest work I have done so far is dispersing or dealing with shame. There is an insidious shame that we don't even know exists because it is so embedded in the culture. It's a shame about being naked, about having a less than perfect or aging body, about masturbating, about having an erection or not having an erection. Part of what I've witnessed with folks on my table or in a class, who are aroused for a period of time, is that those cultural structures of shame come to the fore where they can be recognized for what they are — a con. They are like the Emperor's New Clothes. We all agree to see them, but they don't really exist. Recognition of this dynamic helps allow the shame to drop away.

In addition to running the school, teaching classes, and hospice work, I saw up to thirty private massage clients a week. I booked them back-to-back, and just got into a mode which I called Massage Monk. Often I wouldn't even eat. I would just go for hours. When I was in Massage Monk mode, I was in a wonderful feeling state that eating would have interrupted.

In the midst of all the erotic touch, I began to question my role. Given my background, I couldn't help but think that what I was doing was prostitution. Of course, I had always been taught prostitution was wrong, but something felt so right about it. At the same time, I noticed that certain individuals who attended the weekend classes felt deeply, spiritually moved in the role of the erotic masseur. I began searching for a vision, some name or concept for what I was experiencing in my own work and witnessing in the classes.

That's when I started investigating the ancient sacred prostitute tradition. I learned how what I was doing was similar and how it was different. Sacred prostitutes of the past were part of the fabric of society, part of a temple or church, part of the establishment. They were people, mostly women, who served to embody the divine goddess. Connection with a sacred prostitute was connection with the divine. In 1990, I invited fifty-five men to join me for six days of training and exploration into the role of service as a sacred prostitute. Initially I called this training Sacred Prostitute Summer Camp, but because the word "prostitute" carries such a negative meaning,

> *As sacred intimates, we are a lot like Johnny Appleseed, planting seeds, erotic seeds, expecting results and knowing we've done our best.*

I changed the name to Sacred Intimate Training.

Today's sacred prostitutes are still in service to some vision of the divine, but they are not integrated into society. They work alone. They're outlaws. In my mind, what defined sacred prostitutes then, and sacred prostitutes or intimates now, is that they are present for the highest good of their clients and in service to a greater power. It's all about intention. They are intimate out of compassion, offering a great opportunity for sexual joy, celebration, healing and transformation through this sacred erotic connection. I want to be careful not to define sacred intimacy in a purely therapeutic model because it is more about being a shaman, about creating an environment of hospitality, vulnerability, equality, openness, pleasure and connection so that transformation can happen. As sacred intimates, we are a lot like Johnny Appleseed, planting seeds, erotic seeds, expecting results and knowing we've done our best. We never know exactly what will happen. We can't know the script ahead, but something beckons us to go deeper and deeper into what I call the mystical place; the place of awe. We go because we are compelled beyond resistance. You just have to trust the process, take the next step and travel on.

By the fall of 1992, I felt that my mission with The Body Electric School was complete, so I sold the school to Collin Brown who had been my office manager and had participated in numerous trainings since 1990. Part of what I learned from the Jesuits, and part of what I try to impart in my teaching, is the need for ongoing discernment. In every stage of one's life, one has to discern what his or her gifts are and what he or she should be doing; how to best make use of their time. I knew that the school would thrive in the hands of those I had trained and I knew there were other things for me to do.

One of those other things was to create a teaching video so that I could offer people a way of learning Taoist Erotic Massage in the privacy of their own homes. The first of these teaching videos was called "Fire on the Mountain" which, amazingly, was named by Time-Warner's Book of the Month Club as its sex education video choice. They sold more than 2500 copies in one month! The call was clear. I had educated only about 2000 men in six years of classes! Since then I have been making and promoting many more teaching videos and DVDs. I do this because, in the area of sex, we've not been well educated. We don't know what's possible. We're educated in all kinds of other areas, but not about our own fire; our own eroticism. I'm doing this because most people don't know what their options are. I call for zero tolerance for sexual ignorance.

By the year 2000, recognizing that all of the work I and others were doing with sacred intimacy was flying under the radar, I felt I somehow needed to take the work to the next level. I wanted to bring sacred intimacy out from the underground, out of the closet, into the culture in a much bigger way. I wanted to see this work conjoined with psychotherapy and teaching in a way that would be beneficial for all. You can talk to a psychotherapist about sexual abuse for years, but for intervention on the physical plane, we call on a sacred intimate or erotic shaman. It is in the physical world that the trauma took place and that's where the healing most effectively takes place.

Erotic work needs to move into the open, on the screen so that it can be part of the network of society, recognized for its profound healing nature and as a spiritual path. I want people in the Catholic Church to say, "He or she is on a sexual, spiritual path." This is the next big step. In order to understand and facilitate this, I completed my doctoral degree in Human Sexuality at The Institute for Advanced Study of Human Sexuality in San Francisco in 2002. A lot of psychotherapists and other professionals come to this school—which is the only professional school of sex—to get training in various aspects of human sexuality.

> *Erotic work needs to move into the open, on the screen so that it can be part of the network of society, recognized for its profound healing nature and as a spiritual path.*

After completing my degree, I approached the administration of the school and said, "I think that erotic bodywork—sacred intimacy—needs to be part of your graduate school program. It needs to be available, though not required, for a PhD or Master's degree in human sexuality or public health and sexual education." In the next breath, I had convinced the school and the state of California to allow me to offer a certified course in what we are calling Sexological Bodywork which is a half-trimester, 150-hour course.

When I started the Sexological Bodywork program, I had to stop doing individual sessions because those sessions required a tremendous amount of focus, creativity, and energy which I needed for writing and other academic pursuits. Now once again, I am venturing into doing some one-on-one bodywork sessions.

Joseph Kramer, PhD

My vision today is to see conscious, skilled erotic touch evolve to reach more people and to become ever more effective. I really think we need a system of peer review, supervision and ongoing education for sacred intimates. We also need a national peer body so that we can have a professional affiliation with educational resources, referral services and the ability to network. Tomorrow I may have another vision to build on. There's always another vision.

I had never met Isa Magdalena prior to writing her story. Still, after several hours of phone conversation, I felt comfortable, connected, charmed and seduced in the presence of this almost shy woman who is so passionate about her work. After our initial interview I made several follow up calls to delve deeper into her story. Isa was always gracious and thoughtful—constructing her replies with deliberation. In exacting words, Isa told me that her exploration of erotic touch was born out of her own deep longing to really touch, to touch completely. It also grew out of her observation of the persistent presence of Eros and her relentless desire to understand it.

Isa was also involved in her own writing project, A Map of Sexual Pleasure, *so we began to encourage and support one another, developing a long-distance friendship. It was many months later that I met Isa for the first time and had the privilege of spending several days working with and getting to know her better. Isa is steadfastly passionate about her work.*

PHOTO CREDIT: PK KOZEL

Isa Magdalena

It's been an amazing journey, really. The erotic exploration I started doing first came from my body, but I would also say that there were strands in the cosmic field that were helping me. When I think back, my mind immediately starts to see how those strands converged, leading me to integrate sex and spirit. I seem to have this particular way of stumbling along, picking pieces from here and pieces from there—pieces from various traditions. But ultimately, the way I work is not traditional. Perhaps not having a teacher or a guru gives my discoveries a fresh innocence.

I began working as a massage therapist in a sauna in Amsterdam. In Amsterdam, things are different. Everybody goes to the saunas, which are completely socially accepted. People there are more comfortable about nudity, so we never worried about draping our clients. Not all, but most of my clients were men; they were the ones who could best afford massage. What I noticed very quickly was that the genitals were always there. What I mean by that is that either a man wanted to have an erection, didn't want to have an erection, had an erection and wanted me to pretend not to notice it, or wanted me to do something with it. No matter what, the focus was always there. Either by trying to deny or wanting to emphasize what was happening with the genitals, they were always an area of much attention. In that beginning period, I needed to figure out how to deal with this. I could not simply pretend I was not noticing what I was noticing, nor did I want to. I started playing with moving that erotic charge into other parts of the body. It wasn't really complicated. I simply let erotic feelings rise without touching genitals, because once genitals are touched, they tend to become quite demanding in their need to continue being touched. Then I would go on sensually massaging the body, fanning flames of Eros. Looking back, I'd say that this was perhaps a sneaky way of playing with Eros, but people would get off my table literally vibrating with erotic energy.

I loved to play with erotic charge. It gave me a lot of pleasure and still does, but at that time, before the early 90s, there was no guidance for these things, no language, or at least I didn't know of anything. What I knew was that people either offered "therapeutic massage," which excluded and draped everything erotic, or they offered "sensual massage" and barely touched the rest of the body. I liked it all, so ultimately I simply combined them.

I realize that the cultural climate in Amsterdam has been a very big part of my journey. It never occurred in my mind that I was doing something wrong or unlawful. In Amsterdam, I had learned therapeutic or sports massage, what in the States is known as Swedish massage. I learned to go pretty deep into the muscles, joints and ligaments. I also learned acupressure and shiatsu. Those models, except acupressure, mostly look for pain. If you hit a pain place, then your treatment is good. And that's where you dig just a little harder. Pain was the indicator of good treatment. I used my feet, my knees, and I was pretty strong—people loved it.

At the same time, I noticed that these men would come back every week and nothing had changed. I realized that these people didn't necessarily come to be fixed or changed. Mostly, they just came to have a break from their busy lives and to feel pampered. Over time I began to feel that digging into those places, which were already resistant, was meeting resistance with resistance, and it exhausted me. So I started to experiment with a whole different approach. I began to use soft touch, and found that soft touch went much deeper, because it doesn't barge in with force prompting a natural counter force. I

Of course, you can never touch only muscles. Muscles are always connected with the emotions and the rest of the person.

began to look for the places in the body that willingly let me in, and then by using some juicy sensation, I seduced the more resistant places into relaxation. This way of inviting the body to open through sweet, pleasurable touch was not only highly effective, but it taught me a basic life philosophy I still find tremendously valuable.

It was all very experimental. Years later, I understood that I was using erotic energy from the sacrum and the sensation in the skin to wake up the body. I was aware that the erotic charge fed me, too. I noticed that I was not exhausted like I had been before. I was no longer just the giver and they just the receivers. We were exchanging erotic energy without ever fully playing it out in any conventional way. It was just more balanced and I think that my clients felt that they were touched more completely—deeper. Of course, you can never touch only muscles. Muscles are always connected with the emotions and the rest of the person. I would also say that the massage touched a reviving source in people that I couldn't access without using erotic energy. It was rejuvenating, enlivening—the same way you feel right after having sex, but without the depletion that orgasm can bring.

Except for feeling very connected and learning a lot from my clients, I was quite alone in this work. I longed for someone I could talk to, someone who could understand. Several years later, I met Annie Sprinkle at one of her performances in Amsterdam, and I was just blown away with it. She was my goddess. I thought, "Oh my God, there's somebody who knows. There's somebody who understands!" I wanted to meet her immediately. Soon after, a friend of Annie's named Cora opened a center called the New Ancient

Sex Academy (NASA), and she started to attract sex teachers; Betty Dodson was the first one. When Annie came to teach at NASA, Cora called me and we arranged a massage for her. Annie was very happy with the massage, and she told Joseph (Kramer), "You've got to go get a massage from Isa." This was the beginning of meeting people who had an idea about what I was doing. Meeting Annie and Joseph was extremely exciting—people on a similar path!

After meeting Annie and Joseph, I began exploring Taoist Erotic Massage and the Big Draw with Cora's husband, Willem, who had taken one of Joseph's weekend workshops for men. Until this time, Taoist Erotic Massage had only been applied to men, and we wanted to know if this would work on women too. Willem and I met once a week for several hours. We played with the different techniques, using breath and touch to build and spread the charge. At first, I was very resistant. To me, the breathing was work, too much work. I would get very turned on and I just wanted my orgasm. I wanted sex, not breathing! Then, after about three sessions, I let go of my resistance and really opened up, emotionally and psychically. I experienced sensations I would describe as profoundly cleansing. I cried and I cried. I cried so much. I used whole boxes of tissues. I noticed that after a session with

> *I felt the same kind of opening with him that I felt after the retreats, so I began to wonder if we were working with the same energy, and I believed that we were.*

Willem, my heart felt very open. At the same time I was exploring with Willem, I was attending some spiritual retreats. I felt the same kind of opening with him that I felt after the retreats, so I began to wonder if we were working with the same energy, and I believed that we were. This really strengthened my awareness of the oneness of sex and spirit.

For several years, I was the only woman who had thoroughly experimented with Taoist Erotic Massage and the Big Draw. It was an incredible gift—personally and professionally! Suddenly I had a format or a method for all the stuff that I had been finding intuitively. Joseph's work helped me make the leap to touching genitals in a way that felt sacred and interesting to me, not just arousing. He gave me valuable tools to do way more with those genitals than simply jerk someone off or engage in sex. His method for building the sensation, coupled with the breathing, expanded the erotic energy and gave me the opportunity to work with people in a holistic way. The body wants to be whole. The genitals are not something you can just take off and put on the shelf until you want them again.

Taoist Erotic Massage adds a completely different dimension to the sexual experience. It is a tool that has three main components. The first is the genital stimulation, the second is breathing, and finally the Big Draw. There is a splendid menu of genital strokes that can be used to reach an exquisite state of arousal. Then, instead of riding the familiar train route of arousal straight to orgasm, you use your breath to scoop up the arousal and spread it throughout your body. The breathing adds a completely different dimension to the sexual experience. It is specifically designed to produce the most profound states of pleasure. The breathing can produce a state that looks and feels a little weird, but never mind, let it happen. Sex is about letting go and letting your body do whatever it wants. The breathing assists you in pushing through emotional resistance—resistance to feeling, to receiving. It also keeps you present in the moment, and is the key to spreading the energy throughout the body. After a period of building and spreading arousal, when you're about to explode with pleasure, you go into the Big Draw. Often the Big Draw brings you into an altered state which can be highly transformational.

What we call pleasure is a combination of two stages. First is the excitement stage in which we get more and more aroused; we go up and up and up with excitement. If you kept going like that, you would reach a place of discomfort. So what is needed is the second part, which is the release and relaxation that brings joy and contentment. Excitement alone is not pleasure. Contentment alone is not pleasure. When you combine the two you have "The Pleasure Package"—excitement and release, arousal and contentment.

Sexual energy opens us up and sweeps through our core. I call it the chimney sweeper. Usually we keep our sexual energy localized in the genitals and then it goes out. When we reverse this process and bring that energy into all of our body, our whole system opens up in a way that goes deeper than with any other method that I know. By reaching deeper into ourselves, we access places that have been hidden, opening doors of

> *Sexual energy opens us up and sweeps through our core. I call it the chimney sweeper.*

rooms that we didn't even know existed. When I do the Big Draw, I feel like my entire system gets updated. The tricky thing is that you can open doors of rooms that are too big or that come with psychological complications, and there I think we need to be careful. We really need to be very respectful of our limits.

In Amsterdam, I could be very open about what I was doing, and I was very popular. Once I began to use the techniques of Taoist Erotic Massage, I was able to offer a unique kind of massage, and there were plenty of people who wanted to experience it. But I only stayed in Amsterdam a couple of years after that. I was invited to come to the United States. Initially I was going to be in the U.S. for six weeks, but well, now it's many, many years later.

By the time I left to travel through the U.S., I had already begun offering a workshop on touch at NASA. I didn't really see myself as a teacher, nor aspired to be one, but I did have opinions about touch that I was ready to share.

While traveling, I landed at a gathering on Lama Mountain, a spiritual retreat in Santa Fe, where I met the people who are still very important in my life. In previous years, Joseph had offered his work at this gathering, and they were happy to have found a woman who could offer "sex and spirit" material to women. That's how I was welcomed into giving my first workshop. It was a time of magic, yes, and many nerves too, but I can hardly imagine a gentler and richer plunge than at that gathering. I didn't venture directly into teaching erotic massage in the workshops. Initially, I led exercises in movement, breath, touch, especially soft touch, and in honoring our bodies. I learned the importance of creating ritual for these exercises.

That is one of the gifts I got in the U.S.—ritual. In Holland, I had learned a lot about touch, but I had no clue about ritual.

Ritual, to me, is important, because it creates a container for the mystery we're inviting. Ritual lets us keep one foot on the earth while the other flies, God knows where. I also knew the importance of safety because of the incredible intensity I'd experienced in my one-on-one work with sexual energy. Some people ended up screaming or crying, and all sorts of wild things happened on and off my table. So when I did this workshop at Lama, it was important to me to make it safe for the women to meet themselves erotically—through themselves, each other, through touch and movement and breathing. The workshop, as I did it then, actually became the foundation for the women's basic workshop at Body Electric.

> *Ritual, to me, is important, because it creates a container for the mystery we're inviting.*

Joseph called to tell me about what was going to be the first sex and spirit event to include both men and women. It was called the Cosmic Orgasm Awareness Week, and was led by Joe and Annie. In that week, I connected with Collin Brown who was looking for a woman to teach women's programs. Collin helped give me the framework to do erotic work in a group. I was hesitant about it. In my private sessions, I had been working with such deep intensity. I couldn't see how it could be done in a group. It's not that I thought that women were too fragile or too wounded or too something to be outrageously erotic in a group. That's not it. The men's workshops were very genital focused, and it didn't take them that long to get there. My experience was that, in general, women need a longer or deeper building of intimacy before they let someone play with their genitals. You can't just skip that phase and say, "Honeys, time to spread your legs now!" I tried to go faster, believe me, but women, thank God, protested all over the place. The result was a weekend in which we spent a lot of time building up to the Taoist Erotic Massage, to then finally practicing it on the last afternoon. The downside of this format was that, after we were done with this intense, incredible event, it was about time to wrap up and say goodbye. We often went way past the official time, just to get some decent closure and grounding.

At first, Collin and I butted heads like crazy. It makes me hot when I think of it, and I smile at the same time. My protest was that he wanted women to do the workshop the same way men were doing the workshop, and that really did not work for me. Now I see that some of it also was a different style of facilitation. Collin was very structured and worked with a set plan, whereas I need to improvise and work with what comes up at the moment. Each step we take as a group decides the next step. That doesn't mean we are devoid of a general outline and a common ending place; we just can't quite

> *We also began doing events for couples, because so many excited women were going home after our workshops and saying, "I want my husband to know about this."*

predict how we're going to get there. This, to me, was a way to make space for mystery and surprise, and let participants co-create the event. At the time, I thought this was a fundamental difference between "male" and "female" approaches. Now I think it's just as much a matter of personality, regardless of gender. Eventually, Collin let me follow my own instincts about what women needed.

After a few workshops, women were asking us — my partner PK and me — to do more than what Body Electric was organizing. We also began doing events for couples, because so many excited women were going home after our workshops and saying, "I want my husband to know about this." These groups were certainly powerful. What comes back to me is having a room full of people feeling safe enough to open up in ways they couldn't imagine was possible. I can't tell the number of times women said, "This feels so natural!" referring to being there with other women, taking off their clothes or not, talking about genitals and sex without shame or guilt, and without having to perform for a partner. You know, it is natural. We just got trained out of it.

There are many, many beautiful moments that stand out in my memories from these workshops. I remember, for example, a delightful little transformative interlude when we, a group of women, were in the midst of showing and telling about our vulvas. In one woman's story, the Catholic Church came up. (It seems that the church is never far away when we talk about sex.) Lots of women had Catholic memories, and among the ranting was a lot of laughing. Suddenly someone grabbed her vulva lips and, moving them around, burst into spontaneous song singing "Hallelujah, Hallelujah." Within seconds, we had a choir of vulva lips happily singing "Hallelujah." It didn't feel irreverent. It was purely a celebration of joy, and we didn't have to leave our cunts out of it.

At another workshop, I remember a man bursting into tears after being held by one of the other men of the group. When he suddenly realized the emptiness of that aspect of his life, he started sobbing and said, "I don't know of any tender contact I've had with another man. Not even with my father!"

One of the tenderest moments I witnessed involved a woman who had been torn between staying and leaving throughout the entire weekend. I could see that it was so hard for her to stay and not run away screaming. The workshop put her totally on the edge. To me, she was this delicious person who was so present, and she was often the person I would use as a compass for where to go next. She was my measure of how fast to go, because she was having such a hard time. Ultimately she stayed, and in the very end she said, in a way that I still hold as one of my biggest treasures, "I've never felt so loved before."

When I think about what happened during those workshops, I remember not only the successes, but also the failures. Some things I feel I couldn't quite resolve. One woman wrote to me after a workshop saying that she felt that the approach was too "male"—too goal oriented. And this was after I thought we had restructured it to make it more appropriate for women. Even more shocking was something that came to me indirectly. One of the participants had said to a friend that during the workshop, she was ecstatic—she loved it. But afterwards she wasn't sure if she violated or traumatized the woman she worked with. That has never left me. Those comments caused me to re-evaluate the exercises.

This is not to say that most people didn't come away with a very positive experience, but that it's important to find out what else is needed to take care of people after a workshop. At the time you feel great, but when you come home you can fall into a big hole. It's not that we have failed, but simply that there is much more to learn. We have a serious gap in the process. For this reason, I'm less interested in using erotic energy to generate big cathartic erotic processes until we figure out how to fill that gap. I don't have the answers. Maybe we just need to stumble along for a while until we figure it out, but it's not something to be ignored. If this work can go on, if it can grow, we need to listen to the needs.

It's not about endlessly dwelling on every emotion, but about letting them be part of the journey so they don't turn into monsters. See, generally we have understood that sex is severed from spirit, but sex is also often severed from having feelings. That's why it can happen that one partner is galloping quite excitedly to an orgasm while the other is waiting for it to be over as soon as possible. I believe that the main reason that couples stop having sex is not because their bodies don't want it anymore, but because they don't know anymore (if they ever did) how to reach each other emotionally.

> *I believe that the main reason that couples stop having sex is... because they don't know...how to reach each other emotionally.*

A one-on-one session is quite different from the group experience. It can have more detail in it, and can go deeper, more directly into the individual issues. Over the years I've developed a general formula, but it always has to be adapted to each session.

When I meet with a client, we begin by having a talk so that I can learn what is happening in the person's life. Then it's important to find out what her or his wishes, expectations, and intentions are for this session. When that feels complete, we move into what I call "temple time," or ritual space. Another way to describe ritual is to say we move from particle reality into wave reality, or to say that our logical mind gets a break and our bodies can speak. There is a clear beginning and end to the session; what happens in the middle we can't predict. The beginning is time to tune in. We (the client and I) come from different worlds and now we come together, so we have to somehow meet on the same frequency in a short period of time. The process of tuning in is different with everybody, of course, depending on how well we know each other and what language we share—talking or silence; movement, or stillness or touch. But usually, sooner or later, we will sit opposite each other on the bed or on the massage table. I'll lead us through a simple process of becoming present with our bodies here and now and inviting all our parts. If appropriate, we will breathe together and connect on an energetic level. This beginning usually tells me how to continue into the deep

> *I love sex and I love spirituality. It's very obvious to me that spirituality and sexuality are one and the same.*

meeting. After that, we flow into the body of the session, and that is where the mystery unfolds. Every session is different. I always end with giving thanks for the sharing and the experience, and with un-merging our energies.

This all sounds very serious, but it's often very playful. It's exciting and fun. It's deep, serious, intimate, beautiful play. We connect on so many levels, inviting all our parts to show up and truly meet, filling them with pleasure to then go back into the world. How's that for a job description?

One of the crucial elements in this work has been that, over the years, I have had to learn that a very big need of people is to give touch, not just receive it. It took me a long time to allow people to touch me, to receive them in that way. What I had noticed was a big hunger to be received. Sometimes "please let me touch you" can be translated into "please receive me," which can be translated into "please love me." These people were saying, "Let me in, take me for who I am. I really need you to receive my touch. I really need you to receive my body." Once I saw that, it was a lot easier for me to let it happen.

I have strong feelings about the terms "sacred prostitute" and "sacred intimate." My main objection is that these words still come from a paradigm that separates "sacred" from sex, not to mention "sacred" from the rest of life. I love sex and I love spirituality. It's very obvious to me that spirituality and sexuality are one and the same. The reunion of sex and spirit is part of my personal mission in this life, and as I go along, I seem to meet people who want to join that mission.

I've always been a very spiritual person. My mother is very religious, Calvinist. When I was young, even though the church was declining rapidly, we all went to church and read the Bible every day. Now Christianity is not my place, but I feel that having an awareness of a god has been crucial to creating my spiritual hunger in a time when that hunger seems to be rare. I am very grateful that my mother insisted on bringing us up with that kind of awareness even though none of us are following the church now. My father stopped going to church many years ago, a decision that was completely against his upbringing. It was a very courageous thing to do. Essentially he's a pagan, even though he doesn't recognize that word. He is very much into plants and animals. I got that from my father. My parents are both heretics themselves, really. They had the audacity to leave the extreme orthodox church of their families. That act was very, very courageous. According to some of their family members, they might as well have knocked on the devil's door directly but it was the biggest blessing they could've ever given to their children. Orthodox Calvinism is not a small thing. It terrorizes people through life and death. I admire my parents for stepping out of that.

For me, a key to allowing an ever deeper meeting with people was my spiritual Sufi practice. This practice connected me with a love that was way beyond the personal, the romantic, etc. This connection has been the key for me in being able to share more and more of my self with others. Our meeting is totally personal, and at the same time, it's beyond personal. It's like reaching the universal through the personal and reaching the personal through the universal. This all sounds so terribly intellectual for something so not-intellectual, something that simply feels good.

Along the way, I've also learned the importance of being acutely aware of my own needs and wants. In other words, to know what gives me pleasure as well. I can't afford for the exchange not to feel good — the price is too high. Namely, I end up dissociated, in pieces, or resentful and angry. So, I learned to turn "no" into "yes." Let's say I'm touched too fast or simply wrong. First, I need to notice that I'm cringing and withdrawing. Then I need to find what I want instead. I need to let my client/playmate know what I want. I had to learn that being in touch with myself and standing up for my needs was essential to being able to stay loving and very close. It's not about rejecting somebody or telling the person they are doing something wrong, but rather about finding out what works together. I noticed many people end up in a relationship with sex where there is either a "yes" or a "no." There is rarely a range between. It is either "yes" to the whole package or "no, I don't want any part of sex." With the Taoist Erotic Massage, we can have an enormous spectrum between the yes and the no. At any time during the massage, there is the invitation for each person to ask for exactly what he/she desires. There is also the gift of not having to perform, not having to get somewhere. We don't have to reach a particular goal. There is no way to fail.

In the last few years, I've been working through another layer of my own incest work. This has been an incredibly painful and enriching healing process. It has helped me to understand other people who live with and through trauma.

There was a time when I could not bring myself to do anything sexual, period. I could barely get turned on, so forget about sex and penetration, not even with myself. One of the people I'd been seeing for a long time still really wanted to have sessions, so I agreed to meet with her. There were times when she would get very turned on, more turned on than I, or I would get turned on and then get scared. I would just have to stop and say, "I'm sorry. I can't do this. I can't go any further. All I can offer you is my own impossibility to have sex." Remarkably, she turned the ritual around and approached me in the same way I had approached her, asking, "Where are you? What do you need now? What can we do now?" Later on, she went through her own period of not being able to be sexual. The most amazing thing I find is that for both of us, the most empowering aspect, perhaps, was that we were allowed to say "no" to sex. In hindsight, I can hardly imagine this difficulty anymore. Not because I'm always sexual, but because the range of what "sexual" means has grown so much bigger.

These last few years, I've spent a lot of time writing and coaching. The writing has allowed me to articulate what before was just a feeling. Writing made me see that my sexual experiences didn't fit anymore within the language that was available. I felt that I had to create alternate concepts to give a place for them. For example, the language of sex is usually narrowed down to the physical, because our culture doesn't hold the idea that sex is also spiritual and emotional. Love is everywhere, but the door to this state is inside of us and sex is one of the ways to open the door. I hope other people can benefit from my articulation some day.

Doing sex coaching has given me very concrete insight into the questions people have about sex and what informational gaps need to be filled in. People need answers to basic questions like "how do I best communicate," or "how can I prolong erections," or "how can I ask for what I want if I don't truly know what it is that I want?"

This has inspired me to write *A Map of Sexual Pleasure: Living Sensually and Sexually with or without a Partner.* It presents a way to cultivate these qualities from the inside out. Sensuality is often forgotten, I find. Yet sensuality is the very force that connects inside with outside. And sensuality is the giant area between the all-or-nothing in sex and the all-or-nothing of having a partner or not.

This *Map* goes from cultivating awe when we walk on the street, to breathing into our genitals, to having sexual orgasms, to becoming familiar with sexual energy and its immense power for pleasure and healing. And for all this, we don't even need a partner. I want to offer this *Map* as a guideline to people I work with individually and in groups. And to anyone who's interested, of course.

I hope that people on spiritual paths and people on sexual paths will continue to talk and listen to each other. The process of healing the split between sex and spirit affects the way we live in the world. Maybe, some day, we will allow spirit to come back to earth. Maybe, instead of us thinking that we have to go up to the heavens to find spirit, we will just look around, feel our bodies, our sensuality, our sex, and know that we don't have to go anywhere to be spiritual, but just be here and now.

To say that she is honest, smart, outspoken, courageous, outrageous and funny only partially describes Betty Dodson. When I first called Betty to ask her to share her ideas and experience, I was impressed with her openness and generosity. Later, on a trip to promote the first edition of this book, I had the pleasure of meeting and spending a bit of time with Betty. Again I was impressed—this time by her kindness.

Referred to variously as the "Mother," the "Grandmother," or even the "Godmother of Masturbation," Betty Dodson has been talking publicly about women's masturbation since the 1960s. No one has done more to liberate female sexual pleasure. Through workshops, instructional videos, and groundbreaking books—most notably Liberating Masturbation, *later revised and republished as* Sex for One—*Betty has been a very important agent of change, giving women the tools and the confidence to discover and own their sexual pleasure. In her book* Orgasms for Two, *Betty incorporates masturbation into partnered sex, or as she puts it, "partnersex." Most recently Betty released her memoir* Betty Dodson: My Sexual Revolution.

PHOTO CREDIT: RICHIE WILLIAMSON

Betty Dodson, PhD

Sex, in and of itself, is valid. We don't need to justify it or sweeten it by attaching the words "sacred" or "spiritual" to it. Sex is what it is and it's central to our well-being and happiness. Sex is one of the few times in our lives when the body, mind, and emotions are unified. The moment of orgasm is the moment of this unification when it is all working together and we plug into that big old generator in the sky. That would be my definition of a higher power.

What I'm doing could be called sacred prostitution, but the minute you combine the words "sacred" and "prostitution," you've lost most of your audience. Most folks can't go there because of the word "prostitution." I say we have to start talking plain and to the point, and stop trying to decorate sex with spirituality to make it more palatable. We can simply talk about sex as it is: a fact of life. If someone wants to make sex part of their spiritual practice, that's fine. But how you pray is your personal business. How you are having your best orgasms should be seen as political.

> *We can simply talk about sex as it is: a fact of life.*

Focusing on sexual pleasure and orgasm might seem frivolous in a world that is about to collapse in on itself. However, I think part of the trouble we're in today is because of the scarcity of erotic energy. Sexual pleasure may be the very thing we need to turn things around. So I do what I can. I've spent the second half of my life promoting masturbation as a massive healing force that is largely untapped. I've reached millions with my books and website, and I continue to do private sessions with women because I think women are our best hope. Many of my clients are postmenopausal women because they have reached the point where they don't give a good rat's ass, and they can finally be real.

In 1965, when I ended a sexually diminished marriage, I was sneaking orgasms through masturbation while my husband slept in the same bed. By 1966 I had a new boyfriend and we embraced the sexual revolution. We were having threesomes, foursomes and group sex. Whoop-dee-do! My life turned around completely. That was when I started creating erotic art. Everything opened up, and orgasmic partnered sex was the key that unlocked the door. Having orgasmic sex with a man who was interested in experimenting was like entering the Garden of Earthly Delights.

When I moved from sexual repression to sexual expression, my life totally changed. My self-esteem blossomed. I suddenly had the courage to have an exhibition of my erotic art, and as far as I know, I was the first woman to have such an exhibition. My sense of personal power just kept escalating. In 1974, I self-published *Liberating Masturbation: A Meditation on Selflove* which later became *Sex for One: The Joy of Selfloving*. Publishing a book on the subject of masturbation required a lot of self-esteem and courage. When I was doing all of this writing and educating about solo sex, there were times when I felt like I'd invented masturbation. Meanwhile, masturbation was everybody's favorite dirty joke. Most men thought it was hysterically funny; most women thought it was something only men would be interested in doing. It wasn't easy talking about masturbation, but at the same time it was very liberating. There is so much creative energy in this basic form of sexual expression.

> *...masturbation was everybody's favorite dirty joke.*

All of the pioneering sex educators came from different backgrounds. Kinsey studied gall wasps. Alex Comfort was a zoologist. Beverley Whipple was an RN. Annie Sprinkle was a prostitute. Joe

Kramer was a seminarian. I'm an artist. My fine art background has definitely shaped how I work as a sex educator. It was through mastering the nude in art school that I learned to find my own voice and to create a personal form of artistic expression. Once I'd mastered the nude and I knew I was good at it, I felt able to take on anything. I made the right decision when I left the art world to teach sex. No regrets — today I believe that any teacher who changes a person's life for the better is practicing the highest form of art. When I painted and drew around the clock, I got praise and awards. However, if you're dedicated and creative as a sex educator, chances are good that you'll still be called a pervert! Sticks and stones…you know the rest. I am simply telling women the truth about our bodies and orgasms as I see it. Telling the truth takes guts, but we've got to do it in order to change the way we view human sexuality. Sex is more than mom and pop procreative fucking.

Good sex is like an art form or a set of skills that must be learned and practiced. This is what's missing for most of us. Do you think you could dance the waltz without someone showing you the dance steps? Well, if you think you can fuck without someone showing you how to make the best moves, the results will likely be disappointing. I've been teaching women about orgasms since the 60s — specifically about being responsible for their own orgasms. Nobody gives me my orgasms. I go and get them, and I prefer to be in control of my clitoral stimulation.

If we don't own our own orgasms, we don't own our own bodies; we don't own our own lives.

If we don't own our own orgasms, we don't own our own bodies; we don't own our own lives. This is some radical shit, and by radical, I mean going to the heart of the problem. In my private sessions, I teach women to bring masturbation into their sexual relationships. The reason this is so taboo is because women are still protecting the male ego. Built into most men's estimation of how good they are in bed is a measurement of their ability to bring their partner to orgasm. That's why so many women fake orgasms.

I mostly do private coaching, and rarely teach groups except in lectures. I ran masturbation groups for women for twenty-two years, and in the process, I wore out my hip joints. I had to get titanium hip replacements. When you wear out your hip joints, it's either from being too sedentary or from too much action. Dancers and ice skaters wear out their hips. I wore mine out from masturbating standing up. My private sessions are three to five hours so we can relax and take our time. That's a revolutionary concept right there: taking time for sexual pleasure. I'm a one-afternoon guru. By the time it's over, I've shown you most everything I know to get you started. Then I suggest you forget everything I said and find your own sex style. My success rate is fairly high. Many clients have an orgasm the first time they work with me. It may take a little more time for some, and a few women come back after they have practiced at home. I don't delve into the psychology of sexual repression.

> *Dancers and ice skaters wear out their hips. I wore mine out from masturbating standing up.*

I don't want to explore how we got so messed up, but I do have some ideas about how we can make sex better.

As a culture we are so ignorant about female sexual pleasure. Women, as well as a few couples, come in with all sorts of misconceptions about orgasm. Often, women are trying to get orgasms exclusively through vaginal penetration. Now, in my mind, that's the dark ages of female sexuality. Would a guy try to come from having his balls pulled? Absolutely not! Men go right to the end of the penis to the most sensitive place on their glans, and they stay with it. I say keep the clitoris engaged during vaginal penetration.

The women who see me are usually professional women of all ages. My favorites are women in their fifties. These postmenopausal women are feeling a new sense of freedom. They want to experience more sexual pleasure. I also see women in their twenties, thirties and forties, and some of them are learning about orgasm for the first time.

When a woman comes to me, we first have a conversation, because I want her to feel as comfortable as possible. I speak frankly and clearly, so she knows exactly what we are going to do, so there are no surprises. My work is similar to a personal trainer who shows a client how to use the equipment in the gym. The coaching session begins with a genital examination. I'm still amazed at how many women have never really looked at their genitals! Their lovers may have looked, but they haven't. So I invite each woman to explore her vulva with both hands. I sit beside her and we look in a free-standing mirror together. I might ask her what word she uses to describe her genitals. "Do you like the word 'pussy,' or should we say 'vulva' or 'cunt?'" Anything except "vagina"! The vagina is the birth canal with a minimum of nerve endings. However, parts of the internal clitoris surround the vaginal barrel. The internal clitoris includes the bulbs, legs, and urethral and perineal sponge. Women are going to have to come up with a new name that incorporates the internal clitoris, as well as the inner and outer lips. Everyone can say "vagina," but it's difficult to say "clitoris." If we continue to make the mistake of calling our sex organs "vaginas," then for many women and men, that means putting something inside a vagina should satisfy her sexually. While some women enjoy vaginal orgasms, they are still getting indirect clitoral stimulation. But most women will want some form of direct clitoral stimulation during partnered sex.

If a woman comes to me to learn how to have her first orgasm, or how to have a better orgasm, I explain the importance of breathing and using pelvic movements. I also suggest that she try conscious penetration with my Vaginal Barbell, and work the PC (*pubococcygeus*) muscle against the barbell. Then I observe her while she coordinates all this with her clitoral stimulation. She starts with manual stimulation. Then I'll have her try a little battery vibrator, and from there we go to a softer electric vibrator called the Passionette. Usually we end up with the Magic Wand, the big momma of electric vibrators. If she restricts her breathing or forgets to breathe, I will remind to her breathe. When she stops moving, I remind her to keep rocking her pelvis. Very often, when a woman starts to feel aroused, she freezes up. As a sex coach, I keep her moving, breathing, and working the PC muscle, while she tries these different forms of clitoral stimulation.

I have worked with women who cannot identify an orgasm when it's happening in their bodies. One time a woman had a huge orgasm, and then turned to me and said, "See, nothing happened." I said, "You just had one hell of an orgasm and it was beautiful." Usually if a woman can't identify pleasure when it's happening in her body, it's because her idea of what an orgasm should look like is overly dramatic. She thinks it should look and sound like it does in a porn movie, or like it does for her husband, when he comes and then drops off into a deep sleep. Several women believed they'd never had an orgasm because they didn't feel sleepy afterwards! That's when I explain that when it comes to orgasms, women are bottomless pits! A woman's first orgasm is usually just the beginning! Given the chance, most of us can have two or three or many orgasms. You see, the vibrator doesn't fall asleep. It just keeps going, and a woman can keep going, too.

Some women become afraid when they experience intense sexual pleasure. They will get very high, very close to coming, and then stop. Sexual arousal can feel so unfamiliar that it's scary. Often a woman will say, "I am afraid I'm going to lose control." The experience of sexual pleasure can be terrifying. I felt that way too, in the beginning. Eventually we learn that the only thing we're going to

> *...if a woman can't identify pleasure when it's happening in her body, it's because her idea of what an orgasm should look like is overly dramatic.*

lose is the suffering caused by sexual repression. That's all.

I believe sex coaching is how we will be teaching sex in the future. The Institute for Advanced Study of Human Sexuality in San Francisco has created a course that will certify sex coaches. I think that's great. At first, I wanted to control how people would learn to be sex coaches, but obviously I can't and won't. When I first started writing and teaching about masturbation, I felt like I'd invented it. I can get a little possessive. However, hands-on teaching is too important to be owned. I just want to share what I know.

Goddess bless the Internet. I've had a website since '98. Finally I have a public forum that isn't censored. Women and men need to be educated about their bodies and sexual pleasure, and masturbation is our first natural sexual activity. Teaching "abstinence only" to young women and men is very damaging. The idea that talking to young people about masturbation and birth control will encourage them to do partnered sex is ridiculous. What would help young people put off having sex until they've mastered birth control to prevent unwanted pregnancies is an honest, in-depth discussion of masturbation.

It was Saturday evening at a workshop for exploring and celebrating eroticism. The event for the evening was a costume party, and Steve Howard's tiny room was jammed with half a dozen women trying on outfits from the impressive collection spilling out of his suitcase. There were painter pants and clown pants big enough for two. There was leather wear and sexy men's attire. There were also some lovely feminine pieces, including a sweet pink taffeta number. The room was full of laughter as people tried on clothing and Steve helped accessorize with free-spirited delight. My first conversation with Steve, two days earlier, found me glued to his dark brown eyes. His focus on our conversation was intense; his presence filled with uncommonly generous caring. At the time of our interview, Steve was taking leave from both his private psychotherapy practice of ten years, and his faculty position in the Department of Psychiatry at a prestigious medical school. The fresh perspectives he learned from receiving erotic healing work inspired in him a desire to re-evaluate his life. He saw a new possibility for psychotherapeutic healing as well — a vision of a new combination therapeutic modality that includes psychotherapy, physical touch, and eroticism.

Steve Howard, PhD

Erotic touch, without a doubt, has been the most powerful healing modality I've ever known, and I've had extensive experience with psychotherapy, psychopharmacology, and hypnotherapy. There's something about the psychic depths that this healing has been able to reach that has been very effective in liberating me from shame and opening my heart to love and connection with others. Sadly, sacred intimacy—which uses erotic touch and energy, coupled with hearty doses of spirituality and sexuality, to heal—is a modality that we don't see anywhere in mainstream psychology. We don't even have a language for this. It's simply not on the radar screen.

I've experienced incredible, ecstatic states of arousal from sensual, erotic massage combined with breathwork—what I felt I needed to describe as a whole-body, white-light orgasm. This experience was beyond words in the same way any orgasm is beyond words. It was more extraordinary than anything I have experienced before. That I could reach that state through breath, touch and music—without drugs—was and is mind-boggling to me! A handful of these moments—these mystical, spiritual experiences—shook me to my core in terms of my awareness and belief in another reality. They have opened up my capacity for a deeper spirituality, a more loving reality and a profound communion with God/Goddess. Why this thing, that is so remarkable and has no artificial ingredients, is not a part of adolescent initiation is mind-boggling to me.

These experiences blew the lid off my fears about living anything other than a safe, conventional life so that I now have the courage to make what otherwise would seem like outrageous life decisions. I'm about to close my practice, which I've been very dedicated to and which has been supporting me nicely. I'm about to walk straight into the unknown. I have no idea what I'm going to encounter, but I need to give myself this time to learn what it is that I really want to do with the next part of my life. I might return to psychotherapy or I might do something completely different—something unique.

There are times when I doubt the wisdom of my decision and I become afraid, but I've learned about a place of internal strength and fearlessness, and I draw on that. I've also been inspired by a community of people involved in sacred intimacy that I respect and admire as role models for leading very creative, unconventional lives. These people are capable, well-grounded and psychologically sturdy.

It was intrigue that first guided me, several years ago, to visit a sacred intimate named Heath and explore eroticism outside the context of a regular, private sexual encounter. I was not sure what to expect, so I very cautiously and politely asked Heath, "What is it that we're doing here?" He looked straight at me and playfully said, "It can be whatever you'd like it to be." He wasn't being flip or smarmy in any way. He was being sincere and direct. That simple

Permission to explore without shame was a wonderful gift which I eagerly and gratefully accepted.

phrase was wonderfully expansive. That wide-open possibility of cocreating something between us, something we both agreed to, with no imposed parameters, was completely new to me. Permission to explore without shame was a wonderful gift which I eagerly and gratefully accepted.

I shyly confessed that one of the things I found stimulating was exhibitionism. I was not talking about the lurking-on-the-street-corner style of exhibitionism. I've never found pleasure in being an exhibitionist to somebody who's not voluntarily engaging. I wasn't one to employ it on unsuspecting people for shock value, but rather in private settings with a lover, and yet I was still very ashamed about it.

To my confession, Heath remarked, "Ah, so you like to show off?" When he used those words, it was the first time I reduced exhibitionism to a basic non-clinical form of behaving. His tone of voice was completely non-judgmental, supportive and even playful. Those words "show off" were the key for me in realizing some of the conflicts, the apprehension and the excitement that I felt about exhibitionism.

Extroversion, which can be pretty close to exhibitionism, has always been a big part of my personality. Exhibitionism is a grown-up, sexual word, but showing off came at a very young age for me. I realized that, as a kid, I liked to act and entertain. I was very much an extrovert and was shamed about it. I had carried the shame for a long, long time without realizing it. That first session became a very powerful one for me, because it brought sexuality, talk and open-hearted acceptance together in the same moment. We opened up a new avenue of play; a new way to have fun without feeling conflicted and shamed.

With the reduction of shame came the rediscovery of sex as play. I've acted out a number of my sexual fantasies over the past few years. I have a partner who loves to role-play and is very adept at it. We've acted out many, many fantasies! Whether it's a fantasy of seduction, power, or forbidden love of some kind, it's liberating, empowering, and enlightening. I've discovered a lot about myself through role-play. When I take on a certain character or role, I often get to explore hidden parts of myself. It's also an expansive way to have erotic fun — sort of like high-school-drama-club-meets-sex. What fun to pretend, to play "make believe," and not feel an aftermath of shame!

I've also been having fun doing nude modeling work for several photographers and artists. I suppose the modeling is a kind of role playing. It's definitely acting out a fantasy, since it's something I've always wanted to do but felt too conflicted about. It's been so great to do this in my forties. It's a blast! I feel more sexually alive, vital and attractive than I did in my twenties or thirties. I also feel that I have an air of sexual confidence that people respond to positively. After a period in my late thirties of waning desire, I've rediscovered this pleasurable self-expression which has been revitalizing. It's helped me be in my forties and remain somewhat immune to the liabilities of aging that I hear others express.

Shame is a continuous battlefront for me. I think that I could have shame about cooking the wrong thing for dinner or for using premium gas instead of regular! As a therapist, I teach people to identify when they're feeling shame. Shame is a remarkably potent and often unseen emotion. It is the unseen engine that drives a lot of other unpleasant, self-defeating, negative feelings and behaviors. Shame is actually the operative emotion behind self-criticism, low self-esteem, envy and depression. It's often the root of what people are experiencing. So I try to highlight shame and look at its tentacles, because it's easier to clean out that way.

We live in a shame-based culture where a lot of our child raising is implicitly designed around shaming. Sometimes the shaming is intentional and sometimes it's unintentional. A sacred intimate relationship offers the opportunity to not only talk about issues of shame, but to put the healing into an embodied, experiential realm.

> *Shame is actually the operative emotion behind self-criticism, low self-esteem, envy and depression.*

During one particularly powerful session with a sacred intimate, I had a very erotic and cathartic experience that dramatically changed who I am as a person. That healing reached deep inside me to a place that is beneath words and beyond intellect, and made a change at a level that is very, very difficult to reach. The way I think of what happened is that I imagine myself as a child with a broken bone which was never set exactly right, so that movement, while possible, has been extremely difficult.

I had carried a lot of unresolved guilt, responsibility and grief over the death of my brother who died when I was fourteen. The responsibility I felt over my brother's death existed only in my imagination and my own unconscious world. He died of leukemia; I played no role in this. It was only years later that I realized that

I carried a huge burden of "survivor guilt"—the guilt many of us feel after a shocking or age-inappropriate death—why did I survive and not my brother? By what chance event or random factors did I get to live and not him? And also, on an unconscious level, perhaps this mistaken self-attribution of responsibility came about through my own magical thinking—how many times, as young brothers fighting, had I thought or uttered the words, "I wish you'd die!" Perhaps that had in fact made a difference.

The sacred intimate I was working with was very skilled. Through touch and breath, he led me through altered states of consciousness—at times mystical, at times psychological—and then backed off for me to have my own inner experience. I experienced a lovely, deep, nonverbal healing.

To the world, I seemed imperious and not easily injured. I appeared sturdy, but like many kids (and adults) who look sturdy and interact well in the world, I was extraordinarily sensitive and easily shamed. The truth is that the armature of my personality had been badly broken. I had no choice but to adapt to the abnormal structure of my personality until that moment when something reached deep down inside of me, into a very young, very core place, and reset the break, straightening the armature of my personality. I was left with an exhilarating sense of "okayness." "I'm okay!" It was as if my basic underlying anxiety and fear switched to basic

> *It was as if my basic underlying anxiety and fear switched to basic underlying okayness and self-acceptance.*

underlying okayness and self-acceptance. I made a fundamental shift to knowing that I am a sound, decent person capable and deserving of giving and receiving love. It was as if the hand of God, or an angel, or benevolent spirit, with the skill of an adept psychic surgeon, reached into me and gently corrected something at the level of the foundation of selfhood.

Inspired and infused by this experience, I made an important decision to tell my parents about my experiences of erotic healing and my attraction to it. I had reached a point in my life where it seemed implicitly dishonest for me not to tell them. I had been deepening my involvement with Body Electric, where I was assisting the staff for intensive workshops. I had not yet made a decision to become a sacred intimate, but was certainly drawn to the possibility. I'd say I was in the developmental process of claiming this as part of my identity. How much of my professional identity it would become, I was not at all certain. So I told them, not with the idea that they would endorse it or support my involvement, but because everyone else who was close to me knew of the importance of this, so it seemed that I was lying by omission. Much to my amazement and delight, my parents were not only supportive, but also affirming of my feelings. I was tremendously touched. It was a significant moment; one that I am sure I will look back on years from now as a highlight of our relationship. Because of their acceptance, I came away with a sense of being loved—loved in a cosmic, universal, unconditional way. That's given me strength.

I feel very different inside now after the sacred intimate work I've received. I feel a greater capacity for love, compassion, patience, creativity, playfulness and humility. I feel less shame and fear. My priorities are different. I've traded in the priorities of material security and professional prestige for deepening my relationship with spirit and living more lovingly towards others. Now my focus is on keeping my heart open.

I also find that I'm less judgmental and skeptical about things that I once dismissed as too "wacko" or too "woo-woo" because they didn't make sense to me. I once disregarded anything that claimed the reality of unseen energy fields like chakras or auras, but I've experienced amazing sensations in my body that I can't explain. By extension, I assume that there are many other things, many other experiences that I can't understand, so I'm open to any possibility. I've been disabused of my egotistical, narcissistic belief that I know what is and what is not. I realize that I don't know. That's very humbling and very delightful, because now I look at the world with the eyes of a child knowing that anything is possible. As a result, my practice has been altered in a very profound way. While I'm not including any erotic touch, I am able to be with my clients in a much more compassionate, accepting way that honors their own erotic explorations. I feel that I'm better able to be truly excited and supportive about my clients becoming who they are. I'm far less invested in the idea that I am the expert and know the answer.

> *I've been disabused of my egotistical, narcissistic belief that I know what is and what is not. I realize that I don't know.*

The collusion of an odd mix of forces such as well-meaning feminists, mental health care providers and right-wing politicians has created an atmosphere which is, in many ways, much more phobic about eroticism and much more sex-negative than it was decades ago. The results of uncovering and publicizing how much sexual abuse and trauma exists in the culture were and are of tremendous importance. Paradoxically, and unfortunately, this has contributed to a dramatic pendulum shift towards hyper-vigilance and caution about the misuses of sexuality and the broad brush repression of anything remotely or even imaginatively sexual. For example, in the 1970s, it was considered routine and therapeutic for therapists to offer a hug to a patient if this was intended as a healing act. Today, most therapists would consider giving a hug as likely material for a malpractice lawsuit. Rampant trauma and sexual abuse has forced the culture and the healing profession into thinking that any sex or any touch is suspect. Most mental health professions have very rigid ethical guidelines against any physical contact between patients and therapists. This is why it's impossible to use erotic touch within my current work as a psychotherapist.

It would be so dynamic to integrate all the rich understanding about unconscious functioning and human interactions of modern psychotherapy with the deeper level of healing that can happen through erotic touch.

One of several possible futures I see for myself is using my years of training to forge a new, dynamic psychotherapeutic technique. It would be so dynamic to integrate all the rich understanding about unconscious functioning and human interactions of modern psychotherapy with the deeper level of healing that can happen through erotic touch. This would involve completely dispensing with the imposed, artificial boundaries of what is permissible therapy and what is permissible touch. It would rely on respect and mutual agreement and a trusting relationship. It's possible that I could bring what I've learned as a psychotherapist into my own sacred intimate practice and it's also possible that I would teach other sacred intimates. This fusion would have to be a form of sacred intimacy, because any erotic touch in the current climate of psychotherapy is simply too volatile and too inflammatory. In other words, it is more feasible to bring psychotherapy into sacred intimate (SI) work than to bring SI work into psychotherapy.

STEVE HOWARD, PhD

POSTSCRIPT: My life in the past few years has involved a tremendous amount of travel and moving around. I'm not in any one place long enough to establish a regular practice or rhythm, but I have gone from being a client of sacred intimates to offering some sacred intimate work myself. This has become deeply a part of my identity as a person—as a healer. I offer sessions to people, by referral only—at times for money, at times for free. I now have a certificate in bodywork. I have not been a practicing psychologist for several years, and although I will likely enter into this work again, the break from it has allowed me to feel less constrained about offering erotic service as part of human healing.

Talking to Gina Ogden may be the only proof one needs to know that Eros is life force. She's got plenty of it. In her warm and vibrant Cambridge home, Gina welcomed me into the sacred circle of her world and shared the history of her work. Gina has had a distinguished career as a sex therapist, family therapist, researcher, teacher, and author. She lectures and conducts teleseminars, retreats and training workshops internationally. Gina has appeared in the media from talk radio to the Oprah Winfrey Show. *She has written seven books on women's sexual health, pleasure, and the meanings of sexual relationship. Her most recent are:* The Return of Desire *(2008),* Women Who Love Sex *(2007, 3rd edition), and* The Heart and Soul of Sex *(2006). She's currently forming a network of practitioners dedicated to integrating sexuality and spirituality, and she's writing another book—of course!*

PHOTO CREDIT: MARTHA STEWART

Gina Ogden, PhD

I am a recovering proper Bostonian. There wasn't any sex when I grew up, at least not in my family. There also wasn't any religion or spirituality, but there was plenty of alcohol. I came into the sex field with a nearly clean slate because I had so little experience. I'd grown up alone. I'd been to nice polite girls' schools. I'd been in two boring marriages, so I'd just not been exposed to very much. I realize, as I look back, that I was always looking for the story that wasn't being told. I was looking for the story of women's power in sexuality and it just wasn't there. If women were included in sex research, it was mainly to look at dysfunction—never to look at experiences that are healthy, juicy, mindblowing, soulrocking, ecstatic, and transformational. The DSM (*Diagnostic and Statistical Manual of Mental Disorders*) lists all of our dysfunctions and pretty early on I was questioning, "In order to define dysfunction, don't you first have to know what health and function are?"

I was born in 1935, so my earliest memory stuff is wrapped around World War II which was very much a time of austerity and fear. I grew up mostly alone, with a mother who was well-intentioned, but alcoholic and crazy. She just wasn't very able. My mother committed suicide when I was twenty-two—right out of college. My father left when I was five. He left to join the Air Corps and become part of WWII, but never came back.

I ended up in two terrible marriages because I had no tools to make good choices for myself. It was out of these disastrous marriages (from which I have two wonderful kids) that I finally, in my mid-thirties, got into family therapy. After some time, I thought, "I don't want to be in family therapy, I want to be a family therapist." Once I started training, I realized that nobody was dealing with sexual issues. Then, as a budding clinician, I was faced with questions about sex that I couldn't answer and nobody else could either. I was also running a woman's group with a colleague where we would keep trying to start conversations about sex and nothing would happen.

I went to the family therapy literature and looked under "S," and sex wasn't listed! This was the mid seventies and the sexual revolution was in full swing, but there was a huge void about women's sexuality.

Then I discovered the Institute for the Advanced Study of Human Sexuality in San Francisco. This was in 1978 and the Institute was very new. By then I had two kids and a full practice, but the Institute had this wonderful educational program that allowed me to go for two or three weeks, three times a year, and then continue my studies at home. The program was amazing—absolutely amazing! My introduction to it all was their SAR process—Sexual Attitude Restructuring. The SAR process is something they invented. The Institute feels that to be a sex educator, counselor, doctor, therapist, etc., you need to have experienced a wide spectrum of things so that you're not just sitting there, in your white coat, examining somebody like a bug.

> *If women were included in sex research, it was mainly to look at dysfunction—never to look at experiences that are healthy, juicy, mindblowing, soulrocking, ecstatic, and transformational.*

The SAR process floods you with every variation of sexual behavior imaginable—everything from a quadriplegic describing how he's able to have sex with his wife, to lesbians kissing, to elephants fucking and more. Then you process your experience in small groups. It freaked me out, but it cracked me open. One evening we were taken to a bump-and-grind burlesque at The O'Farrell Theater where there were some very young Asian women dressed in feathers and not much else. I witnessed these women being plucked at by men and it was just so yuk—so demoralizing! I found myself sobbing in the corner.

The Institute's process was great in some ways, but just as I discovered that there was a big piece missing in family therapy—sex, there was also a piece missing at the Institute—women, or any kind of raised consciousness about women. We were taught to count our orgasms because orgasm is how Kinsey defined sexual health. But no acknowledgment was given that women's orgasms might be different from men's. Women at the Institute protested, saying things like, "We can't count our orgasms because we don't know where they begin and where they end."

> *We can't count our orgasms because we don't know where they begin and where they end.*

What really put me over the edge and spurred me to action was an animal behaviorist who came to the Institute to show us these amazing films about a macaque monkey troop. He had created sexual dysfunction in these monkeys by putting males and females into separate cages. They looked rather forlorn. The poor monkeys just sat there, ungroomed, depressed, knuckles dragging on the cement—like some of my clients, actually. He went on to describe how he and his team had "cured" the induced sexual dysfunction in the male monkeys—but only in the male monkeys. Well, some of the women in the class asked, "What happened to the female monkeys?" He answered, "We don't know about the female monkeys. We don't even know if female monkeys come to orgasm or not. You see our protocol does not include females." He made an assumption that the males were the only ones worth looking at but I was hearing something very different from both clients and colleagues. I was hearing stories about women's sexual response that just did not fit into the research that was being done or the books that were being written. So, this set the stage for my dissertation. I determined that I would focus on women's sexual response: the health, not the dysfunction

My dissertation was titled, *Perception of Touch in Easily Orgasmic Women during Peak Sexual Experiences*. I was laughed at. My advisor was Wardell Pomeroy, one of the authors of the Kinsey Reports, and he scoffed, "Where are you going to find fifty easily orgasmic women?" I answered, "Everywhere!" I asked my sample of fifty women questions about their perception of touch all over their bodies, including genital, but also extra-genital. I asked them if they had ever come to orgasm by extra-genital touch and at least half of them said, "Yes, yes!" I also asked, "Have you ever come to orgasm without any touch at all?" One woman said, "Oh yes, I call that 'thinking off.' I do that all the time." These were questions I asked, but they weren't necessarily questions I originated. They came from clients and colleagues. These questions originated out of women's lives. This was quite different from the hundreds of previous studies which focused on frequency of sexual intercourse and orgasm, as if these were the sum total of the

> *...sexual response begins long before we get into the bedroom and continues long afterwards...*

sexual experience. The conversations that ensued from these questions were filled with color and light and activity—way beyond what you could count or measure.

On a personal level, I began to have extraordinary sexual, emotional, and spiritual experiences of my own. This was partly triggered by my work and what was going at the Institute, and partly by falling in love with the woman I am still with thirty years later. Intellectually, I began to realize that I had a brain, which I never believed I had. I had been an unremarkable student. I remember going to Esalen for a week with a friend and just felt alive in a wonderful way. I thought, "I want to start writing about this stuff. I need to write about how women experience sex." I started writing about my interview experiences, and through a few steps and missteps in the writing and publishing world, wrote *Women who Love Sex*, which is now in its third edition. I wanted to tell a women's story about sex; a story about how sexual response begins long before we get into the bedroom and continues long afterwards to energize our whole lives.

> *I began to realize that we could change the culture if we could change the names we use to describe women who love sex.*

Women Who Love Sex got a lot of press because of its outrageous title. The perception was that it must be about women who love sex too much—so-called sluts and whores and bimbos. It became kind of a cult book for certain kinds of men—most of whom were disappointed once they got beyond the title and actually opened the book.

There was a story of a woman in a dead marriage, a story of a lesbian, a story of a woman in her seventies, and so on—stories which I used to illuminate the myriad facets of women's sexual experiences. I would show up to present the book and there would be men looking for the women-who-love-sex-too-much, but there were many men and women who actually got what I was saying. I began to realize that what I was doing was launching an idea—not just selling books. I began to realize that we could change the culture if we could change the names we use to describe women who love sex.

Like everything else in my childhood, spirituality had been left out so I went searching.

While I was waiting for the book to be published, I made a video of seven women talking about what they love about sex, which I would show when I taught or presented the book. Once, at Emory College, before I showed the video, I asked, "What are the names in the culture that describe women who love sex?" I got the usual—"sluts," "whores," "bimbos," etc. After the video presentation, I asked, "Having seen the video what would you call these women?" Then, I heard "powerful," "beautiful," and "funny." The last person to speak was a man who said, "I know this sounds silly, but I'd call them angels."

It was 1995, I was on the road with the book and people were saying, "You know, the women in this book are talking about sex, but they are also talking about spirituality." I thought, "Bingo! This is so interesting." I decided that when I got off the road, I would do another project and write another hot book on sexuality and spirituality. Then I realized that I didn't have a clue how to define spirituality. Like everything else in my childhood, spirituality had been left out, so I went searching. I tried a little yoga; I tried a little Roman Catholicism, Wicca, a little this and a little that. I found that after two or three weeks of each, I forgot to go back for more. Then I ended up with a knee problem — a really terrible knee problem — and went to an energy healer. Working with her opened me up to the idea of shamanism — which led me to a workshop with Oscar Miro-Quesada, a Peruvian curandero. I was hooked. Interestingly, my father's family is from Peru! I had grown up without access to a father and suddenly I had a way to relate to my heritage through spirit. I took to the practice, which remains a strong part of my life today, and which I ultimately incorporated into my practice of sex therapy and research.

Meanwhile, I was still pursuing the notion of sexuality and spirituality. The field was still being defined by a few individuals, mostly men, using very limiting methodology, and basically talking about their personal responses. It felt like the proverbial blind men describing an elephant. I realized that no one had ever done a survey to get a larger picture. So, I put on yet another hat and started talking to scientist friends to learn how to do a scientific survey. This was the late 1990s, just before the days of email, so I handed out my four-page survey at speaking engagements and I got about a thousand responses. Meanwhile, *New Age Journal* contacted me and asked to publish the survey. Yes! When they published it, it seemed that their readers felt permission to write their own stories, and so by letter and by fax I collected shopping bags full of survey responses and stories. I thought, "Oh my God, now I have to do something with this data!" I didn't have enough money to continue, so I did my two-syllable chant, "MAH-KNEE" (Mo-ney) and almost instantly, *New Woman* magazine called to ask me to write an article for them. I said, "Fine, I'll do it if you pay me an obscene amount of money and publish my survey in your magazine."

When the dust cleared, I had collected a total of 3,810 survey responses and almost 1,500 letters—684 from men, but mostly from women, ages 18 to 86. I had one of the largest surveys ever collected and the only nationwide survey to investigate sexuality and spirituality, but I had no idea what I was going to do with it. I went to the ocean, where I get a lot of my answers, and the ocean said, "Take it to Radcliffe." So, I secured a visiting scholarship at Radcliffe and followed that with two more years of academic visiting scholarships at the Wellesley Centers for Research on Women and Harvard Divinity School.

> *I also found that sexual satisfaction levels went up with every decade of life. The fifty-, sixty-, and seventy-year-olds in my sample were having a better time than the twenty- and thirty-year-olds!*

One of the most interesting things I found out during this period of academia was that the first sex survey, ever, was done by a woman: Dr. Clelia Duel Moser. Between 1892 and 1912, she surveyed 45 wives. What was so remarkable about this was that the narrative answers from Dr. Moser's survey were absolutely parallel to the narrative responses I was getting a hundred years later—a lot of women enjoyed sex! The sex that women loved was not characterized by intercourse, but by multidimensional experiences, including body, mind, heart, and spirit.

After three years of working in academic institutions, I was sitting with an enormous amount of data and trying to grapple with it all. What these surveys and letters were telling me was that sex is much more than physical. Sex is not just about orgasm or anything you can count or measure. Sex is about body, mind, heart and spirit. My survey respondents were also saying that sexual satisfaction is embedded in relationship; relationship with self as well as with partners. Most remarkably, I also found that sexual satisfaction levels went up with every decade of life. The fifty-, sixty-, and seventy-year-olds in my sample were having a better time than the twenty- and thirty-year-olds! This flew in the face of everything we thought we knew. What these respondents were saying was that they had outlived the societal constraints—"good girls don't" and "real men score." They had outgrown the abuses, indignities and disappointments or their earlier lives. In other words, they grew up and took responsibility for their own experiences. They learned to appreciate what they had, even if they'd lost their physical prowess or the kind of desire that makes you want to tear down cement walls to get each other and act like an alley cat. There is something so

> *I was right there, inside the historic or mythic time when there was no separation — sex and spirit were one.*

delicious about ripening, mellowing and reclaiming one's own sexuality. I'm not saying every single respondent felt this way, but this was the trend.

Were my survey questions biased? Of course! Ever since I decided to do my dissertation on easily orgasmic women and then write *Women Who Love Sex*, I was always looking to expand the limits of what's possible instead of looking for what's wrong, so of course, my questions were biased. There is no such thing as a truly random sample—especially when the subject is sex, and one of the great traditions of research is that we study ourselves. We study what we need or want to know. The myth in scientific research is that it has to be objective. There is no such thing as objective data.

So there I was, immersed in academia with my data and my conclusions, and I was really, really tired. I had enough of the research and academic world. I needed to start teaching—but how? Suddenly, I found myself at the confluence of a number of high-energy events. *Women Who Love Sex* got dropped by its publisher, so I decided to bring it out by myself—self publish. It got picked up by Book of the Month Club and Quality Paperbacks. Then Oprah called—I got on *Oprah*! In the midst of all this, I was still trying to wrestle out a way to teach this material—the intersection of body, mind, heart and spirit. The survey was titled "Integrating Sexuality and Spirituality" and suddenly the perfect acronym rose off the page—ISIS. Isis is the Egyptian goddess of motherhood, magic and fertility. She is known as Goddess of a Thousand Names and Initiator into the Sexual Mysteries. Her story is that she sprouted wings and flew all around the earth searching for the thirteen pieces of her husband, Osiris, who had been hacked to bits by his evil brother, Seth. She found twelve of those pieces and reconstituted him, but the thirteenth piece—his penis—had been thrown into the Nile and eaten by a fish. So Isis reached into the red Egyptian clay and created the first dildo, placed it on Osiris, mounted him and created their son, Horus.

The title, ISIS, was strikingly perfect because this survey, and in fact my whole professional life, was a process of traveling far and wide to find the pieces of our lost story and then reconstituting them into the whole. This all came together in an instant! I was right there, inside the historic or mythic time when there was no separation—sex and spirit were one. If you go back into any of the ancient teachings, you see that sex was part of religious ceremony and religion was part of sexual ceremony. This is what I have been doing and teaching and writing about ever since.

I had the name, the Goddess, and I also had a model—the ISIS Wheel. The model had been there all along in my shamanic practice—the ISIS Wheel was modeled after the Medicine Wheel, an ancient template for growth and change. The ISIS Wheel is not a proscriptive or prescriptive model. It's a tool help us understand our personal stories and paradigms. I use the Wheel to parse or diagram the components of a person's sexual world.

In a group circle, which is how I love to work, I ask each person to bring two objects—one of which represents a part of their sexual story they want to keep, expand, grow, or feel better about, and another that represents a part of their story they want to move beyond or transform. We come together in sacred space, into a ceremonial circle that can contain all these aspects of our sexual stories.

Then we introduce ourselves to each other through these objects. Someone may bring a grenade to represent the rage they feel about someone who abused them, and also bring a mango to represent the luscious sweetness they feel with their new lover and so on. By the time we've finished our introductions, we are surrounded by the energy of everyone's stories and everyone's power objects and medicine pieces—very powerful. The energy is tangible. If there are twenty or thirty people in the group, there are that many stories!

One story that I love to tell is about a woman who came to one of these gatherings in Kansas City. She didn't know why she'd come. She'd just driven along with two friends.

Into the circle she placed a knitting needle. Her mother, a working class-woman in pre-pill days, had tried to abort her with a similar needle some fifty years earlier. That's all she had to say. She later pulled me aside to tell me that she had a condition. She didn't know the name of it, but when she described it I knew it was vaginismus, a condition that causes the muscles in the vagina to contract so hard that penetration is painful or impossible. She had a new boyfriend. They couldn't have intercourse, and she was very upset about it. I told her that this wasn't an area of my expertise, but I promised that when the workshop was over, I would send her the name of an MD in her area who could help.

That evening we did a drummed shamanic journey to contact the Keeper of the Flame of our sexual energy. This woman came out of her journey and said, "Oh my God! I've never meditated before. I've never journeyed before, but while you were drumming, two Beings came to me and gave me specific instructions!" She was to forgive her mother whom she had not seen for twelve years, and who was now in a nursing home in the clutches of Alzheimer's. She was to bring tulips to her mother and call her by her Dutch name. She was to go into the top drawer of her bureau, pull out the wedding ring her father had left her, put it on a chain and hang it around her mother's neck. After the workshop, she followed these instructions exactly. She knew her message of forgiveness was received when a tear rolled down her mother's cheek. She took the tear and put it to her own eye. Later, she wrote to the group saying that "the pain was gone from the planet" and that she and her boyfriend had had "a merry dance round the Maypole."

My interpretation of this transformation is that once she fully worked through her emotional and spiritual trauma, her body was able to let go. I can suggest that a woman make amends with her mother, but there's much more to it than that. The power is in the resonance of the group, the ceremonial circle and the magic of the shamanic journey. There's also group support that bypasses the doubting mind, breaking down the limits of transformation. This is a situation in which the spirit informs the physical body. It also happens that the physical body informs the spirit. That's how the ancient sacred prostitutes worked—through the body into spirit. Sexual experience may manifest as orgasmic, with muscular contractions and all of the physical sensations that go with that. Sometimes it's ecstatic, which may or may not include contractions, but may be an experience of profound clarity, transcendence or connections with deities, spirits or guides.

Right now, I'm in the midst of launching an ISIS Network,

beginning with a website of practitioners who are doing ISIS work—thinking ISIS thoughts. What ultimately happens will depend on the group that forms and will develop from the resonance we create with each other and beyond each other. I do know it will be much more than the sum of our parts and that it's part of a very long lineage.

When I think about sacred prostitutes, I think about taking someone into the ceremonial circle, into the inner sanctum—the temple, the crypt—the body. I think about entering into the holiest of holies—body, mind, heart, and spirit. There are no answers to how this all happens—desire, Eros, sexuality, spirituality—it's all akin to natural phenomena like the weather. You might ask *how*, but you don't ask *why*—it just *is*. We're still looking for the word that includes it all—sexuality and spirituality. When you say, "sex and spirit," it automatically suggests a split. Maybe the word is ISIS. Maybe the ancients had a word. I'm still learning—still trying to do my part. On one of my recent trips to the beach, I lamented, "What am I going to do now? Oh, I can't do all this. It's too much!" Suddenly there appeared a line of priestesses before me saying, "You're not doing this alone, don't kid yourself."

> *...desire, Eros, sexuality, spirituality—it's all akin to natural phenomena like the weather. You might ask how, but you don't ask why—it just is.*

Nubia is a desert divided by the river Nile. Homeland of Africa's earliest black culture, with a history that is traceable back to 3100 BC, Nubia overlapped parts of today's Egypt and Sudan. The modern inhabitants of this region still refer to themselves as Nubians. Poor soil, limited rainfall and high temperatures have made it difficult to support a large population for long periods of time. Nonetheless, ancient Nubia was a land of great wealth. This wealth included gold, ebony, ivory, incense and a rich spiritual tradition. "My name, Ren ~a Nut Tmu-Ankh, means Great Star Mother Birthing the Seed of Eternal Life who comes to life as Butterfly Dreaming," explains Nut Butterfly, an ordained Nubian, Khamite ceremonial priestess. As with everyone I interviewed for this book, I asked Nut's permission to use her words to create this story. She thanked me for asking and reminded me that asking is an important part of ritual — the vehicle through which she works. Nut creates erotic ritual for healing and growth. It was a pleasure listening to her silky voice during the hours she shared her wisdom with me. Nut interrupted our interview several times to lovingly attend to her young son. Even a Nubian Priestess must answer the call of a six-year-old.

PHOTO CREDIT: SECRET GARDEN PUBLISHING

Nut Tmu-Ankh Butterfly

I don't call myself a sacred prostitute. I don't call myself a prostitute of any kind. I don't sell sex. I don't sell anything. I am a healer, and you cannot buy healing. You cannot barter for healing; you cannot command it; you can only surrender to it.

I have had my own doubts and struggles. I was raised in the same society as everyone else. My upbringing tells me that working with sexual energy is sex work, and sex work, even with the intention of healing and growth, is still sex work and that makes me a whore. So I dodged this work for seven years—but you can only fight divine destiny for so long. I had received the training, the spiritual, logistical and physical training through initiation with my teacher. I had everything I needed to teach, and so I began to teach, cautiously, in an extremely underground way. A person had to go through three or four priests before they could get to me.

There are a couple of converging lines that led me to do what I do today. I was about twenty-four, and I was at a point where I was tired and literally sick of fighting the energy I had always walked with. My grandmother was a well known root worker who practiced out of our house, so having my own platoon of spirit guides was not a weird thing for me. In spite of that, I had always run from anything that smelled of spiritual guidance. Everything changed when I attended a holistic fair that was being held near my house. It was convenient and it was free, so I decided to go. It was there that I met my teacher, my Baba, and it was in his presence that I got a spontaneous, direct experience of spiritual guidance. It was emphatic, insistent and so clear that I could not deny it. One of the basic tenets of African spiritual culture is that "possession is the law." That is to say, there is nothing that we know that does not come to us by direct divine spiritual possession. Books are fine and teaching is fine, but the truth comes from the source, from direct experience with the divine, such as I had that day.

Also at that time, I was just beginning to heal from rape. I had been raped twice by people I had known and trusted, and though I thought I was dealing with it, I really wasn't. I didn't go to counseling. I was too arrogant for that. What I was wise enough to know was that I had real serious sexual trauma "stuff" that had not been resolved, and that I had to reconcile the split in my experience of touch in order to heal. I had to be able to experience pleasurable, safe touch with a man, so I decided to seek out a professional massage. I found someone to work with who gave me a regular massage, a normal, non-sexual massage, but what happened energetically was like making the most ecstatic love. It was incredible! This happened before any initiation, and though it wasn't designed to be, it was my first sacred, sexual awareness training.

I was initiated at the Temple of *Kra Ptah* in New York City, which has been active for nearly forty years. In the beginning, I was trained in cultural awareness; cultural education. I was taught things about ancient Africa that are rarely taught. I was taught to see the world in a new way, with the center of that world being ancient Africa. One of the ways this happened was that my teacher or "Baba," Sen Ur Heru Ankh Ra Semahj Se Ptah, the elder high priest of *Kra Ptah*, turned the map of the world upside down so that I could begin to see the world from a new perspective. To live a totally African-centered perspective in a world that is built on Western thinking inspired a major shift in my consciousness. The gift of this was that I was able to really open my mind and see many things in a new way.

This is a great teaching tool which I often use with my initiates. When an initiate comes to me, I say, "Let's make a new world." I surround them with new sights, new smells, new sounds and new sensations. I change their sensory world to create a time and space where they have the potential to create new thoughts, new beliefs, and a new way of being in the world. I deliberately refrain from referring to those who seek healing with me as "clients." Instead, all who come to me are called and honored as initiates. Addressing them otherwise dishonors the sincerity of their seeking and the value of our healing mission together.

There were and are many, many initiates. Anyone can take this training, but so far I am the only one to use the training as I do. I was given the very secret sexual training of the Nubian culture, *Sh'ti Mer Iz*, which is described as a sexual alchemy practice to awaken and apply orgasmic energy awareness for body, mind and spiritual healing. The teaching is held very close; it is very special.

Ancient Nubia stretches from modern-day Kenya to the northern edge of modern-day Egypt. The western year 4240 BC is the date that we call "Year One." That's important to me, because it tells me that our ancient ancestors knew that our most fundamental act of worship and our connection with that through-line of the infinite within us is our orgasmic core: our awakened conscious love. Love, not as an emotion, but as an absolute power. What I teach is *Sh'ti Mer*. I playfully call that Tantra's lost great, great grandmother.

> *...our most fundamental act of worship and our connection with that through-line of the infinite within us is our orgasmic core; our awakened conscious love.*

In my tradition, the typical initiation of a woman into sexual mastery has the young initiate surrounded by a sisterhood for the purpose of grooming and training her in the knowledge of her body, and in the knowledge of a man's body. A priest or group of priests would then enter and participate in the initiation, but it is always the women who create and maintain the sacred space. The sexual act is only part of the initiation. A young man would be trained in all of the intricacies of his body in the same manner as a young woman. This training, also by women, of a young man is particularly important to balance his energy. A man must acknowledge the feminine in himself or he can become destructive. A young man understanding the sacredness of touch must understand that the healing touch of a man is just as important as the touch of a woman. He has to be comfortable with that, because he has to be able to relate to his brothers. He has to be able to hold the hand, arm, back, etc., of a man with an equal degree of tenderness and respect that he does a woman's. Awakening a young person's sexuality is more than just acknowledging hormones on the rage. It is consciousness awakening. This is truly divine stuff—God stuff—we're dealing with.

I use ritual to open a time and space for something that is already there. It becomes possible to move out of ordinary thinking and feeling when we create extraordinary time and space. I don't create sacred space or orgasmic energy. I simply bring awareness to the omnipresence of orgasmic energy. Orgasmic energy is around us all the time. What is amazing is that we are, at any time, ignorant or unaware of it. That is an amazing feat. Or maybe it's not so amazing. It is very difficult to hold this stuff as real and true when you are living in a world that says it's not.

> *Orgasmic energy is around us all the time. What is amazing is that we are, at any time, ignorant or unaware of it.*

Orgasmic energy — it's just pure life force, and while we do the best we can, there are no words to truly, adequately describe it. It is just energy. Touch is a very important part of this energy — a beautiful, delicious part. But if you focus only on the touch, then it is too easy to throw off the erotic experience as purely physical, and locate it or restrict it to a particular time, place and person. It's so much bigger than that. So when I begin working with an initiate, we have to do a lot of basic cleansing before we ever get to touch. There is a lot of self-love and self-touch that has to be done. We have to clear away shame and self-hatred. We have to get to a place where they can look in the mirror and love themselves. I ask questions like, "Can you look at your thighs, your breasts, your legs, what's between your legs, and adore and worship yourself?" These are important keys. There is so much that has to be done to unlock and open the doors to the absolute glory and infinity of what's inside of sexual desire, what's inside of orgasmic awareness.

A lot of this basic work can be done via the Internet, although I have discovered that I hate typing, so now I work primarily over the phone. Talk is essential and effective. The talk itself is a kind of initiation. The talk brings us into a common ground of language and focus. No matter what seems to be the problem, we start with talk. For instance, when someone comes to me and says "I'm not orgasmic," I begin by asking them when and where they do feel a lot of joy. We focus on what works rather than what appears not to work. We find out what does light them up; what does turn them on. Is it finding a great pair of shoes? Is it watching the home team win a game? Is it walking along a river? Then I ask, "Where do you feel that in your body?" The idea is to increase awareness of delightful experiences.

I will also look for what it is that blocks the possibility of feeling delighted sexually. Does he/she feel ugly or angry or unseen or fearful? We're looking to understand what lies at the core of the person's experience. Once we understand, then we can begin to relate to it, not with logic or with words, but just with love and unconditional loving touch. Love is really the only tool I have in my tool box. It's the only thing that works, and I believe it is the only power that is. I just need to find the things to love on, that's all. I discover where someone is alive and then focus all the attention on that.

> *Love is really the only tool I have in my tool box. It's the only thing that works...*

Orgasm is not a mechanical process or experience. It is an energetic, spiritual experience. I'm a spiritual healer. My conviction is that the spirit rules the body—not the other way around. I'm a guide, a divine intermediary. I literally turn people on. I'm turned on, I turn you on. That's my job. I'm not talking about titillation. Being "turned on" does not mean "getting off." It means really turning on and really staying on—for life. Being turned on is how we can be in our bodies and have infinite awareness at the same time. It is so appropriate that we refer to an orgasmic climax as "coming." Homecoming is how I think of it—coming home to source.

Every encounter is different. A person has a need and as they begin to express that need, I see how to respond. It's like a key fitting in a lock. There was a beautiful man I was blessed to work with. He was very stressed out. He had no interest in the esoteric or energetic parts of what I had to teach. He was just hurting. Initially, I worked with him online. He began to tell me his story, which is a common one. He was having trouble in his marriage. He was not getting his sensual, emotional or erotic needs met. In an effort to keep peace, he had avoided approaching the subject with his beloved, his wife, but by doing so he had created an emotional and spiritual wall between them. He was, and still is, very much in love with his wife. He wasn't interested in going out and having an affair, and so he was left with this gigantic hole. This lack was causing him to doubt the fundamentals of himself as a human being. He described feeling the erosion of his sense of wholeness. He didn't realize that once the erotic connection had fed him in a way that helped him feel whole and capable in the world, and now that was gone. His ability to do his work was suffering, so his business was suffering. His ability to speak up for himself was suffering, and he was suffering. He even had trouble with very simple things like asking for the right order when the wrong food was brought at a restaurant. This person, this man, who had once been very decisive in the world, had become a doormat—incredibly disempowered.

…water can draw out memory. It can draw out emotional and spiritual toxins.

After a time, we met and I interviewed him to determine if working with me physically was what he really needed. Not everybody needs that. For some people, it's the worst thing in the world because they just go off to some escapist place. For him, the physical sessions were right. What I decided to do was to build all of his sessions around him receiving. This man was a person who wanted to give, give, and give. His identity was wrapped up in his ability to provide, so we used the sessions to help him learn to receive acknowledgment and adoration, to accept that the world desires him. I hoped he would learn to accept that there is love available for him. During each session, I created a sacred bath ceremony for him, and he allowed me to wash him. He was surprised by the profound transformation he experienced from that simple ritual. I wasn't. I believe that water has certain detoxifying capabilities. I believe that water can draw out memory. It can draw out emotional and spiritual toxins. So I was not surprised by the transformation, but he definitely was.

Our first "hands-on" training was simply learning how to give a real hug. Then he learned that he had the power to ask, with respect, for what he wanted and to expect to receive that. We created a space where he could begin to see that it was okay to ask for me to do certain things. This can be hard—asking and expecting to receive. I did not allow our sessions to become a substitute for what was missing at home. I made requirements of him to be emotionally and spiritually present at home as well as with me, because I wanted him to integrate what we did with his life at home. My basic teaching for him was to receive, receive completely for himself, then to take a piece of that back to his wife. My initial instruction was for him to offer her things like a hand massage or a foot bath. He was to stay away from any "hot spots." Soon, he and his wife actually made love for the first time in two years. He was able to reach her using a lot of the things that I taught him. We made a lot of progress; good things happened.

One of the key things I taught him, as I've taught others, is to discover the wisdom within. Everything you need is right inside of you. There is no book, no teacher who can give it to you. You already have it, but it requires a frightening responsibility to wake up to that knowledge. You can't defer to a higher authority when you know that you already have the highest authority.

It gives me solace to know that this, this teaching and initiation isn't new. It's only been a short time in our history that we haven't educated and initiated our young people. That people have grown to age in a state of ignorance as we do now is an anomaly in the human story. My job is to bring about orgasmic awareness; to function as a counter-balance to the denial-induced unconsciousness so prevalent today. Orgasmic awareness means having an awareness of this ever-present energy. Most of us are just kind of deaf, dumb and blind to it until we get titillated, and then we're enslaved by it. We have an unconscious, automatic response to sexual stimuli because we don't have awareness, and we don't have awareness because we have our puritanical denial of all things sexual. If our response is something that we choose, then it becomes a point of knowledge and power instead of a handicap.

Working with couples is like being a midwife to a marriage. It is such a privilege, and it can be great fun! I always start by guiding the couple to speak clearly and to listen attentively, beginning with good basic verbal communication. Then I have them be quiet. I have them simply look at each other. I give them hand movements, a series of strokes to communicate through touch. Again, I often use the ritual bath, having the couple wash each other with loving intention and honor. Wet is good. The flowing, sensual quality of water permeates everything, and it relaxes every muscle. It's a very good start. Next we might move from the bath into some form of touch—maybe a massage. Now, with this groundwork laid, they can open to the heart space of joined orgasmic awareness.

My training with couples is to teach them how to rely on that joined orgasmic awareness as the catchall for everything that can possibly come up in the marriage. Whether the couple is struggling with some argument or trying to manifest something new in their relationship, this is a very good place to begin. I always use real issues when I am working with a couple. It is important that this stuff is real. If there has been an ongoing argument, I have them hold that big issue, whatever it was, that necessitated the weird and off-the-wall step of bringing this woman (me) into their bedroom. This is not what couples commonly do, and certainly not what they do when things are going really well. If they are seeking help, then there are problems!

> *There is no greater mind than that between the thighs of orgasmically alive women!*

Privately, I work primarily with men and with couples. When working with women, I prefer to bring them together in groups. Working one-on-one seems like cheating or short-changing a woman. There is a wonderful synergy that happens when women get together—talk about a master mind! There is no greater mind than that between the thighs of orgasmically alive women! In the Nubian language, the word for knowledge and the word that describes the female sex organs is the same word—"shi tet."

Nut Tmu-Ankh Butterfly

Artist, whore, porn star, academic, teacher, author, revolutionary and activist—Annie Sprinkle is all of these. Annie, who earned her PhD from The Institute for Advanced Study of Human Sexuality in San Francisco, is featured in the Museum of Sex in New York City, and rightfully so. The creativity and volume of her work is remarkable. Few people have ever done so much to help the world reclaim Eros and restore innocent joy to sex. She is the quintessential "Sex Positiva Diva." When I first spoke with Annie, she had just returned from a challenging European tour where she performed her famous Herstory of Porn *multimedia show. As often happens, she was loved by some but maligned by others. Annie was tired and suffering from a sore throat, but still generously agreed to spend some time with me. Talking with Annie was a delight. She has a humble, loving way of expressing herself. As we talked, Annie balanced the exchange by asking me about my own life and our conversation took on an unexpectedly relaxed intimacy. We might have been two women having a late night, casual conversation about almost anything.*

PHOTO CREDIT: JULIAN CASH

Annie Sprinkle, PhD

My parents were very intellectual, liberal Unitarians. They were not sex negative, but not very open either. They made sure I saw the films about babies being born and about menstruation. I'm sure if I had asked my parents for more information, they would have given it to me, but I was just too shy—excruciatingly shy. So I knew something about reproduction, but nothing about sex except what I learned on the playground—it was going to hurt. (It never did.) When I was relieved of my virginity at age seventeen, I found out that I liked sex! I was delighted. I thought "Oh, my God, this is great! More people should know about this!"

By the time I was eighteen I was working as a prostitute! One of my girlfriends was working in a little massage parlor and she invited me to come in to answer the phones. I had no idea that I was really working in a whorehouse. After a couple of days, I was asked to start giving massages which led to sex, and I joked that I was just a horny masseuse. It took me a couple of months before I realized that I was a prostitute! That might have been very disturbing, but it really fit my needs, which were to be touched and to feel sexy (I thought I was ugly, thought I was fat, thought I wasn't sexy). I could never see that there was anything wrong with what I was doing, so being a prostitute was a positive moral and political choice for me even though it was illegal.

I was so excited to learn about sex and that learning has turned into an adventure that has lasted more than twenty years! My parents, especially my dad, were very political, very compassionate humanitarians. They were involved in civil rights, and I think that has definitely shaped my work. Compassion has probably been my greatest gift. Well, compassion and big tits. Sex was healing for my customers, and it was healing for me! Most of the time it was fabulous! I saw how the sexual contact relieved stress. I saw myself as a kinky, sexy Mother Teresa. I was spreading my love and having a good time. I thought I was doing a service. Men, mostly, occasionally a couple, came for all kinds of reasons. They might have been physically or emotionally scarred or handicapped. They might have had difficulty finding a girlfriend. They were often interested in trying something new, something kinky, or they were simply stressed and looking for a way to unwind. The sex was really a small part of it. What was more important was the talking, the acceptance, the emotional support, loving touch and just making them feel good.

I was especially drawn to the more difficult, less desirable clients. The ones who were considered ugly were more interesting to me than the good-looking guys. Those clients stimulated my empathy and opened my heart. When my heart was opened, I got more turned-on! I was the classic hooker with a heart of gold. When I share how it was for me as a sex worker, that I actually enjoyed prostitution, most people can't believe it. They can't or they just don't want to. They want to make all sex workers into victims or predators, and admittedly there is a lot of dysfunction in the sex industry, but there is also a lot of wonderful, loving work being done which is beneficial for everyone.

> *When my heart was opened, I got more turned-on! I was the classic hooker with a heart of gold.*

In the seventies, few prostitutes were open about their work and a lot of women lived double lives, but I was "out." I had no shame about what I was doing. I had "whore pride," so I became involved with the prostitutes' rights movement, which was very small then. I'm still very active with outreach and education through such organizations as Call Off Your Old Tired Ethics (COYOTE). We've worked hard—though without success—to decriminalize prostitution. We've also worked to protect the rights of all sex workers, and to educate both sex workers and the public about sex work and its issues. Occasionally, I lecture at colleges on why we need to decriminalize prostitution. Everyone would actually benefit from decriminalization—the workers, the clients, the police, the taxpayers, everyone. After all, prostitution is legal in Nevada and it works pretty well. We'll get there one day.

Joseph Kramer has been one of my best teachers and supporters, and the world's greatest friend. He even asked me to marry him once! We were in Central Park, on a horse-drawn buggy on Valentine's Day. We actually considered having children together, but ultimately decided not to because he's really a gay sacred intimate, and I'm really a lesbian artist and sex activist. Still we have a lifelong commitment to each other, and I consider him my hubbie.

> *I think of sacred intimates as the health food of prostitution, and then you've got quickies for fast food, and you might find gourmet fare in high-class brothels when you pay big bucks.*

Joe coined the term "sacred intimate." I like the term, because it implies a heart connection, but I don't think of sacred intimates as being so very different from prostitutes. The differences among sex workers are kind of like the differences in restaurants. I think of sacred intimates as the health food of prostitution, and then you've got quickies for fast food, and you might find gourmet fare in high-class brothels when you pay big bucks. I know a lot of sacred intimates and a lot of prostitutes. I think that the difference lies in the intention, not in what a person does. I'm fully supportive of all that sacred intimates stand for, but I don't want to put those who call themselves sacred intimates above those who call themselves whores. There are some awesome, fabulous, big-hearted, brilliant whores who are phenomenal sexual healers. They are the embodiment of divine "sex positivity."

All of my work, everything, has been about promoting positive, healthy sexuality. I did one-on-one sex work for twenty years, then branched out into theater and teaching. In 1993, I was at my sexual energy peak. I was an orgasm organism! My sexual energy flowed constantly throughout my entire body. I studied and practiced Tantra pretty seriously. All my chakras were spinning. About this time, I started facilitating sexuality workshops for women. The focus of these workshops was the Taoist Erotic Massage ritual. It's very powerful stuff! I've worked with Joe Kramer and on my own. My passion has turned to exploring and teaching Ecstasy Breathing, which is based on the Fire Breath Orgasm from the Quodoushka tradition of Harley Swiftdeer. I've been teaching what I call Super Sex Technologies, which are techniques to build, move and utilize sexual energy.

I start with exercises that help develop an understanding of what energy is. Having a better mastery of your own energy translates into having better, more satisfying sex. Through exercises, I deconstruct lovemaking into various components such as breath, movement, touch, sound, time, thought, and even risk taking. Then we work on ways to build energy, such as Mantak Chia's Microcosmic Orbit breathing or Kegel exercises. Finally we spend about forty minutes doing erotic breathing which involves breathing in a specific pattern and making sounds. We add in hip undulation and hand movement to fan energy through the bodies. Eventually, everyone goes on a little ecstasy breath trip. We climax with a Big Draw, and finally dissolve into a group afterglow which is a very powerful, very fertile altered state. There are often visions and insights in that state, so it's important to let people linger there. I practice Ecstasy Breathing regularly. I've studied with great teachers all over the world, and this is the best technique I've ever learned for becoming conscious of energy, building it and moving it through the body into a full body orgasm. It's a chakra enema and a shamanic journey—very psychedelic. And it's legal!

I wasn't so interested in working with individuals one-on-one for a long time, but now, after teaching groups for many years, I've become interested in it again. I've been offering sex life make-overs and personal coaching for people who want to learn about sex or have some issue about sex. This takes me back, full circle, to a more intimate way of working, but no matter what the context, no matter what I do, it's always sacred prostitute work. My work is always learning more about sex and then teaching others what I've learned.

> *...but no matter what the context, no matter what I do, it's always sacred prostitute work.*

Perhaps the most interesting, most important work I've ever done was my theater performance piece, *The Legend of the Ancient Sacred Prostitutes*, which climaxed, both literally and figuratively, with a masturbation ritual on stage. Contrary to what some might think, my reason for performing this ritual wasn't to satisfy the exhibitionist in me, but to recreate the ancient temple and to honor the sacred prostitute. To perform this ritual on stage was so perfect! Theater came out of ritual and theater is a ritual. When I began working as a prostitute, I was inspired and felt so connected to this long lineage of incredibly powerful women that I wanted to tell their story.

Women, and sometimes men, from thousands of years ago, in exquisite temples in Mesopotamia, Egypt, Sumeria, Greece and many other places around the world, devoted their lives to learning the art of sexual ecstasy. It was a great honor to be a prostitute. To those men and women, sex meant something very different than it does today. Sex was used for prayer, meditation, ritual, healing and magic. If there was a war, a plague, if people were sick or dying, or if the crops weren't growing, all the people would come to the temple of the sacred prostitutes. An elaborate ritual would be performed where the sacred prostitutes would go into a state of sexual ecstasy. It was believed that when the temple priestess was in a state of sexual ecstasy, she was connecting to the divine, and in that connection she was able to gain knowledge, wisdom, and to create miracles. Some people today call this sex magic.

For this performance, I wore a costume that was designed from a dress I saw on an ancient granite statue of a Sumerian priestess when I visited the Temple of Delphi and the brothels of Pompeii. During this performance ritual, the stage became an altar where, among other things, I lit several candles. With each candle I made a wish, which was also an intention or prayer. Then I invited the audience to make wishes of their own. Just as the ancient sacred prostitutes did, I went into sexual ecstasy to take the prayers or wishes to the divine. It was a rather bizarre and intense encounter, where the audience reacted in every conceivable way. Some people got disgusted or angry, but some said that they felt filled with love and compassion. Others have reported some orgasmic experience—some profound insight or physical healing. Often women cried. That was the most touching response. It was very powerful and very magical when that happened. I've learned a lot about sex and about life from this work. Out of everything I've done, this performance has been the most profound, most educational and most challenging.

I just got back from a five-week tour in Europe performing *Annie Sprinkle's Herstory of Porn*. The tour created tremendous controversy in Norway and Belgium. It provoked thought and conversation—a lot of conversation! There were anti-porn feminists outside the theater yelling and Christians handing out flyers! It's not my intention to upset people, but it is provocative—very challenging to the social structure. It gets people thinking and that's good. On the other hand, there was this eighty-five-year-old, very conservative-looking Belgian woman at one of the shows. I thought she'd never make it through! I thought I'd surely lose her during intermission, but she stayed through the second half. She happened to walk by me as I went out into the audience after the performance. I said to her, "My God, that's so great, you came! Have you ever seen porn before? I hope this wasn't too much for you." She gave me the sweetest kiss on my cheek, and said "No, that was my first time, but don't worry—

I made it through the Second World War." So that put things right into perspective. A moment like that is pure beauty.

That theater experience is not so much about celebrating, but about being touched by the truth. It's about having a deep personal experience which may be sad or scary or transformative or ecstatic. It is always different for different people.

Once, as an experiment, I held a week-long workshop for women called *Metamor-phosex*. The idea was to share some of the profound experiences I've had as a sacred prostitute on stage. Twenty-seven women signed up for the workshop, which culminated with the opportunity to perform sex ritual in a theater. I taught them about the ancient sacred prostitutes as well as some basic Tantra, erotic massage and Ecstasy Breathing. At the end of the workshop, they had the opportunity to sign up to be included, in some way, in the performance. They could masturbate, receive or give an erotic massage, bathe one another, do a Tantra exercise, or just sit with the audience and meditate. I also asked them to dedicate the performance to something they wanted to create or let go of in their lives. These women created a very, very powerful ritual, building huge sexual energy to beautiful music and theatrical lighting. Then we brought it all to climax with a group Big Draw. Boy, we raised the roof! Imagine sitting right in front of twenty-eight women going into ecstasy! Many of the women stayed connected after this performance, and some even went on to do more

> *Sex is so amazing! Sex is a gift — a treasure chest that's available just for the taking.*

sexually-oriented performances. One woman, who owned a tropical fish shop, ended up making a funny kind of erotic magazine for tropical fish owners! I'm not kidding!

Sex is so amazing! Sex is a gift—a treasure chest that's available just for the taking. Sex is ultimately about expanding consciousness, about self discovery, and about going beyond everyday reality to that magical place, somewhere over the rainbow, where we feel divine. We are capable of having great pleasure, having fulfilled ecstatic and joyous lives. We are capable of feeling whole and sacred in these moments.

Annie Sprinkle, PhD

I had heard of Alex Jade's edgy work leading erotic workshops, and read some of her writings on Sadomasochism long before I met her. Alex could be described as a "head turner," but not in the classic sense of the word. She's tall and slender, with short salt-and-pepper hair. You might easily mistake her for a man at first glance, but you'd be compelled to look at him twice. Alex describes herself as "gender fluid," meaning she moves easily on a continuum from masculine to feminine. A shape shifter, one moment she's delicate, seductive and inviting; the next moment she's powerful, regal and penetrating. She is always striking and graceful. Alex has a master's degree in social work, training in movement therapy, and is a licensed massage therapist. In addition to her private practice as a sacred intimate for all genders, Alex teaches sacred intimacy through the Oakland, California-based Body Electric School. Alex also studies and teaches Tantra. She was eager to talk about being a sex worker and about her vision of sacred intimacy as it is evolving today. Alex's words came charging out from the starting gate.

PHOTO CREDIT: KOBALT

ALEX JADE

Sacred intimacy is so new! We're calling on an ancient wisdom, but we're creating something very new, right now! It's evolving out of a blending of many skills such as somatic therapy, psychological counseling, Tantra, Taoism and other spiritual wisdom, so that we have a brand new, dynamic healing form. I really think that as sex workers tap into the vast healing potential of erotic energy, the therapeutic skills of modern psychology become more and more important. I get referrals from therapists even though erotically touching someone totally flies in the face of every established teaching of modern therapeutic psychology. It's taboo! It's heresy! This is the work of the new sacred whore, the sacred intimate, and it's very exciting. We're explorers, scientists building a new body of knowledge.

A lot of therapists use open heart and open mind, but I also access my erotic energy and share that openly with other people. I'm not a surrogate or a sex therapist. I use erotic energy as the healing medium. My body is open. It's not about me exchanging my sexuality with another. It's about me being a channel for divine erotic energy. I'm open to spirit moving through me.

People come to me with a whole range of desires and problems that look very dissimilar but have a common core. Someone might come to me because they're not orgasmic, or because they carry childhood wounding about sexuality, or they might even come to learn more about being a skillful lover. But the common thread is that they come because they are seeking aliveness—spiritual, full-bodied, emotional aliveness. This culture suffers erotic amnesia. We've forgotten how to feel with our whole bodies, how to feel delightful in our bodies. Many clients simply need to learn how to give and receive pleasure.

> *This culture suffers erotic amnesia.*

When a client comes to me, we begin with a body-based exploration. We might start with some breathwork, some movement, or tension release through stretching and massage. We build on that to develop more body awareness through touch. It's important that we co-create the experience. My clients understand that they are taking personal responsibility for what unfolds as we explore together. Depending on what needs or desires are expressed, we might begin to explore more involved channels or paths like erotic massage, or sadism and masochism, or psychodrama. We identify an intention and a plan. Every session is a sacred ritual, and there are threads that go from one session to the next so that we create a healing path.

Being a sacred intimate can be risky, personally taxing, and lonely at times because we're isolated. Sacred prostitutes don't work in the temple anymore. We no longer have each other's nurturing support, so burn-out is a real problem. We have to be very mindful about our own bodies and erotic energy to stay really clear and strong. We need to take extremely good care of ourselves. We have to. It's not self indulgent; it's a necessity.

This work doesn't pay terribly well; there are no benefits and no paid vacations, but it is absolutely compelling for me. I've always been a spiritual person. I've always known that. I was raised Presbyterian, but in college I tried out other churches. I knew something was missing for me. I remember sitting in church one day thinking, "We need to be doing this tribally and moving with erotic energy. Can't we dance with our hands on our cunts right now?" So I started questioning how I could pray in a way that included everything, all of me. I had a pretty high sexual drive and I wanted to know why something as important as our sexuality was being repressed. I was also a body-based practitioner. I

> *...I started questioning how I could pray in a way that included everything, all of me.*

was doing movement therapy and massage therapy, and I was deeply curious why even the body-based therapies omitted eroticism.

In 1990, I met Tom Hammond, who organized the Body Electric workshops in the Seattle area. Tom told me all about this school for erotic education and celebration, and I thought, "Finally, there are groups of people doing this work!" When I became Tom's massage therapist, I learned a lot about eroticism simply by working on his body, and I wasn't even doing genital work.

Tom was living with AIDS. He was using erotic energy as a healing force, as a way to keep his body full of life so that even as he was dying, he was completely present and open hearted. It was exquisite! Tom's erotic energy wasn't genitally focused. He channeled the energy of my touch deep into his body and spirit. I worked primarily on Tom's chest. It seemed to help him breathe better. He had lesions on his skin, and I would focus love on every little feature of his body. I was totally making love to him, not in any conventional way, but making love just the same. We were like honey with each other, so sweet and intimate. That's the kind of enormous, glowing love we shared—just a big love affair from that very deep spiritual place. I worked on him two or three times a week and when he was dying I spent hours with him every day.

The last time I saw Tom, he said that he wanted to spend the day alone, because, in his words, he wanted to be with the ecstasy of his dying. As I walked out of his room, he waved to me and said, "Good-by, Beloved." That's how I remember Tom. He was beaming. Later that day, I went to a park with another of his friends, and we did a ritual to release him. I've never been afraid of death since.

When I chose the name Alex Jade, I'd sometimes say Alex T. Jade, and use Thomas as my middle name. I miss him so much it aches.

It was through Tom's dying that I met his friend, Collin Brown, and became involved with The Body Electric School. Suddenly I was connected to an erotic legacy, and I wasn't alone anymore. I was totally turned on and lit up. Once I found out about other people exploring erotic energy, there was no turning back for me. I was also deeply grieving Tom's death, and I knew that the way for me to heal that grief was to carry on his vision and to dip into the healing power of my own erotic energy.

Tom died in 1992, and I was diagnosed with cervical cancer in early 1994. That was a maturing period in my life. With my cancer and so many people around me getting AIDS, life got real serious, real fast. I thought, "I'm too young to be dealing with death all the time. I have to find some pleasure." It became clear to me that I would die if I did not live up to my full erotic capacity.

I had picked up an STD, human papillomavirus (HPV) when I was eighteen or nineteen. What this meant was that I could no longer have unprotected sex with anyone, not even with my partner. Emotionally, that was very hard to accept, and I did a lot of grieving about it, but physically, the HPV presented no problem until I was sexually assaulted at the age of twenty-five. When I went in for an exam, post-rape, they found that I had dysplasia on my cervix. They were just abnormal cells, not yet cancerous, and I really wasn't surprised that my body would have some serious response to what had happened.

For the next ten years, I endured every allopathic, homeopathic and naturopathic remedy known in an unsuccessful attempt to get my cells to return to a healthy state. In addition to the conventional procedures prescribed by my oncologist, I was putting all sorts of herbal concoctions up my vagina on the advice of two naturopathic doctors. It was a long, long process with no positive change except that I learned a lot about my body. Then, after all that effort, things went from bad to worse. I developed a cancerous tumor. It was so scary!

Because of the level of body information I learned in those ten years, I knew I was carrying a tremendous amount of repression, tension and congestion in my pelvis. I had a very strong sense that I had to increase the energy and blood flow in my body. I just knew it, so I began to pay attention to what I ate and how I exercised. I took better care of myself. What I wasn't doing was getting any rich erotic stimulation. I was caught in a relationship that was erotically flat, stagnant. I knew that I had to be more sexual. I had to follow the erotic burn that was stopped up in my body. I made a choice to try to heal myself through deep personal erotic work.

I broke up with my lover and unleashed my sexual appetite. I learned about Tantra and participated in the first Body Electric event for women. I let my desire flow and purge the rape out of my body. I allowed myself to be far more orgasmic than I'd ever been. Amazingly, the tumor shrank! I'm delighted to say that I now have a healthy cervix, and I didn't have to have a hysterectomy!

There's no one way to heal. That's just the way I did it. That's what my body needed to do. I believe that, especially for those of us who don't release feelings easily, surrendering to erotic flow allows us to metabolize and cleanse the pain we carry inside.

My whole life changed when I was faced with that "live or die" question. When the answer was live, I decided to live very differently. I made a commitment to explore eroticism, especially the G-spot, because I started to understand that the G-spot is the psychic garbage can for all of our past traumas. Trauma, shame and suppression create a tremendous amount of tension in the pelvis, causing physical and energetic blocks that can be very toxic and can cause disease. Once the G-spot—located in the middle of our second chakra and accessible only through deep breathing and deep erotic touch—gets ignited, the energy flows. That energy can purge out all the garbage and our bodies can heal.

> ...*G-spot is the psychic garbage can for all of our past traumas.*

Sadism, masochism and power struggles fascinate me. These primal forces exist in the human psyche, but we lack knowledge about them. It is essential to identify these forces and, instead of driving them into the shadows, bring them forth so that we can use them for healing. If we refuse to give them expression, they can become dangerous. With the right intent, love and acceptance, we can harness these energies into liberating, healing, healthy expressions. I'm discovering some terribly exciting opportunities for clients to experience true surrender through rituals of Sadomasochism (SM) when these rituals are done with consent and love. I recognize that this is very provocative, and it isn't for everyone, but for those people who are turned on by this kind of sexual play, it can be a fantastic resource!

So many of the people I work with express a hunger for a greater sense of connection. They are starved for the feeling of belonging to something greater than they are. They are seeking a spiritual connection. To experience that deep connection one has to be willing to surrender, to trust, to let go of control, to let go of knowing the future. Something essential and important happens when a person surrenders. This can be achieved through prayer, chanting, meditation, fasting, dancing or many other means. The Native American Sun Dance Ceremony is a great example of how someone can be driven to surrender through extremely strong sensation or pain.

I can take someone to that place through sensory deprivation and bondage. When a person is very tightly held and restrained so that they no longer have to hold anything, their bodies can totally relax. They don't have to work. They don't have to do anything at all. They have nowhere to go but totally inward into a womb-like state, into that very clear place. There they can listen to their own knowing, their quietness or their loudness, and know the truth of what connecting to spirit is for them.

One way of surrendering to the divine is in relationship to another person in a power exchange. If you invite spirit into you, to guide you, then you have to be willing to let go of control of your life and be guided. That's not something that happens by thinking about it. People have a nearly impenetrable resistance to giving up control and power. In SM play, a client creates a contract with me wherein I assume some role of being in control and they agree to surrender. When they surrender to my will, it gives them a sense of the sweetness of letting go and trusting another. By completely letting go into my hands, a client learns to trust letting go into the hands of spirit. By letting go of how they will be guided and just being open to what emerges, they can let spirit guide them through me.

Sacred intimate work is about being in holy relationship. It doesn't necessarily matter what we do or say. I think that some of the best healing happens simply because there are two human beings together. Spirit is individually in me, but also I'm part of the big picture, the big "Oneness." Spirit can be exchanged through my body, my thoughts, and my energy. Relationship is the medium of that exchange, and it's through this exchange that we can become more whole—more holy. Being in relationship replenishes. By understanding my body and by moving sexual energy through my body, I can turn up the exchange between another and myself, and turn up our connection to Oneness. One of my central tasks is to be in relationship with other living beings like the earth, plants, minerals and people.

My work can make close relationships difficult. My partner, my beloved, has to be extremely mature and open. I'm a sex worker! It's terribly challenging for her, so I try to be very sensitive to her feelings. It's a difficult thing to be with me knowing that I touch a lot of people intimately—sexually. I can't share who my clients are or what I do with them because of confidentiality, but I do share how I am affected by my experiences. She knows that these people are not my lovers, they are my clients. I don't spend the night with them. I always practice safe sex. I take a shower before I come home, and I come home, every night, to her.

My partner is very grounded, solid and loving, which really helps her to be able to support my work and me. Still, it's hard, so we spend a lot of time processing and really communicating with each other. Consequently, my work has continued to strengthen our relationship and our spiritual connection. Our life together is unusual in some ways, but we also spend a lot of "normal time" indulging in simple pleasures like hiking or rock climbing or going out to the park to watch the sunset. Whatever the outing, we include sushi, always sushi.

All my siblings know what I do, but it took me a long, long time to come out to them. First, I came out as a lesbian. Then I was working with people with AIDS, and now I'm out about my erotic work. I have family members in key public and social places, and I felt it was my obligation to let them know what I do so they wouldn't be surprised. The first person I chose to disclose everything to was my brother. Now my sister knows what I do, but I don't think my father knows. He knows I work with sexuality, but I think he believes I work with gays and lesbians to empower them sexually. Nobody asks questions, although last year my sister confessed that she looked me up on the Internet. My family is quite conservative, so accepting this in me is definitely a challenge for them.

I often find my own challenges in this work. Last year, I was approached to work with a man who told me he was sexually turned on by young boys. Wow that sent me reeling! It really, really pushed my buttons. I thought I was open and accepting. I thought I'd seen and done a lot of outrageous, kinky stuff, but that definitely pushed my boundaries. That desire did not fit into my value system. Still, I wanted to help him, so I had to avoid getting caught up in whether

I morally condemned or accepted the desire. Condemnation wouldn't make his desire go away. To do my job well was to be present with love and to help him unravel the underlying story.

I decided that I had to become very curious, so I did a lot of reading. I got a lot of counsel, a lot of support, and I did a lot of reflection. I realized that a person expressing that kind of desire has some arrested sexual development (usually around the age of the object of attraction) that prevents them from reaching sexual maturity. They are erotically stuck and they need to go into that stuck place to seek healing. I came to realize that it was okay to play with that imagery as long as it was not actually with an underage boy.

We're erotic beings from the day we're born. It's normal and it's healthy, but five-year-olds need to have five-year-old eroticism. It's damaging when that gets entangled with the eroticism of an adult. I worked with him to fully express his fantasies through role-playing. Traditional treatment for this kind of sexual desire is often to repress it and shame the person, but by really bringing his feelings out we were able to understand the source and directly deal with his issues. In doing so, we took the charge out of his fantasies, kept him from acting inappropriately and hurting someone. For me, this was profound evidence that if we take it off the streets, out of the shadows into sessions, and approach it with love, we can create a powerful avenue of healing.

> *We're erotic beings from the day we're born.*

It's really gratifying for me when I can problem solve in this big way. When I embrace complex erotic challenges and help people through intense emotional experiences, my brain gets turned on. It's actually a full-body turn on. I like that! Every client is different. With some I get an instant, juicy, sexual turn-on. With others I really have to struggle to find a way to be with them, but I can usually find a way to do that. I have a pretty extensive erotic palette.

My dream is to have more sacred intimates working in partnership with psychologists, social workers, allopathic doctors and other healers…

I know that everyone deserves pleasure, and I feel that my work is better when I can genuinely be turned on with a client. If I'm having difficulty connecting with someone erotically, I try to look at the situation from a therapist's perspective so that I can understand what's going on. I look at my own triggers. I try to find a way to make each situation work, but I do have to be true and clear with myself. For instance, if someone is being really aggressive with me, I might refuse to work with that person or refer him or her to another sacred intimate. I'm also aware that I have my own natural erotic ebbs and flows. In the winter, I'm a little caved in, and that's okay. I can still offer my clients good work; it's just that my own eroticism is subdued.

The path that's emerging for me is stepping more into leadership. I'm developing my confidence and mastery of this work. I feel like I've gotten through the first door of understanding this knowledge. I really understand erotic energy in my own body. Now I get to take that knowledge into the realm of teaching and training. My dream is of the bridgework that could happen. I have a master's degree in social work, and hope to be invited into that community to educate other mental health workers about sacred intimacy. My dream is to have more sacred intimates working in partnership with psychologists, social workers, allopathic doctors and other healers to move this work to the next level. Imagine the community we could build and the healing that could happen!

Julie's story may be unique in the specifics, but the theme is classic. Her story is the struggle between the essence of her individual nature and her need to find a place of belonging in the tribe. It's a personal story of transformation through working with a sacred intimate, and like so many stories of transformation, it is hard to describe logically. For Julie, a talented sculptress, this was a particularly challenging task. Her language is form; not words. We talked for quite a long time to tease out the words to describe her journey.

JULIE BERGER

My yearning to explore bondage was very animal-like—a primal instinct. Before I entered those temple gates, before I knew what a wonderful gift I was going to be handed, I was a very different person. This transformation has been huge. It wasn't so long ago by the calendar, but by the measure of change in me, it seems like a very long time.

Very nervously, I phoned Alex Jade one day and nervously expressed to her that I had this yearning, this desire to explore BDSM. The voice on the other end of the phone said, "Its okay, I'm more than willing to help you explore this." Wow! What an extremely positive, pivotal experience that was for me. It took me from a place of fearing that most people's reaction would be one of judgment and rejection to "Yes, you can do this!" It was such a breath of fresh air for me.

> *I still held a deep fear of opening up to my own sexuality.*

In spite of this initial positive experience, I was very fearful about meeting Alex and of moving in this direction of exploration. I still held a deep fear of opening up to my own sexuality. I had my own judgment. In my mind, my desires were wrong—perverted. I held my own great shame about my yearnings, compounded by my partner's harsh critique. But when

Alex opened the door and I was warmly received, it was like going to the temple.

Alex and I began exploring, in conversation, how I had arrived at her doorstep and what I desired. I told her that I was living with a very interesting paradox. I grew up in an environment where I was rarely restricted. I had, in many ways, a wonderful, rural upbringing. I was allowed—encouraged—to express myself openly. I remember when I first started working with Alex, I described my upbringing and she said, "My God! You came from a healthy family!" But because my family let me run so free and wild, I had to relearn things when I went out into the world as an adult.

In my family we communicated honestly, really honestly. If we didn't like something, we said so and sometimes we said so very emphatically. Sometimes we yelled at each other. When I entered into some of my first relationships as an adult, I found out that speaking my mind honestly and yelling didn't work in my favor. It didn't take too many episodes of this to figure out that I had a lot of unlearning and conforming to do. That was hard for me. Conforming is a real stretch for me, and though I work at it, I will never be able to be "in the box." I mean, it's impossible. I try. I conform a little, but then I think, "Okay, what are my rewards? Is there a benefit to conforming? How do I meet another in a way that our culture has prescribed and stay true to my essential nature? How do I stay honest?"

> *The bondage immediately took me very deep within, into the depths of my innermost creativity.*

It seems I'm always doing that dance of tension between culture and essence. It's the same dance I do between my sexual desire and what I think our culture condones.

Alex and I talked about how this tension sets me up for an adversarial and confusing relationship to the world which demands restrictions. We talked about both my need for containment and my resistance to that. I was hungry for clear, irresistible limits that give me no choice but to give up the battle between desire and limitations. Part of me longs to be contained, and yet part of me gets very angry when someone attempts to restrict me. What that feels like in my body is overwhelming, scattered energy and anger.

Once Alex had an understanding of my background and of my longing, we decided to try an exploration of bondage. It was amazing! The bondage immediately took me very deep within, into the depths of my innermost creativity. I found that being in bondage forced me to surrender, and that allowed me to go inward in a way that I had not experienced before. It allowed me to slow everything down in myself, and brought all of my energy to one small point. It was a very powerful meditation.

It's not that there was something inherently wrong with the energy that I was feeling in my body. It was electrical and positive most of the time. But it was also really, really big and difficult to direct or focus most of the time. I learned that bondage could help me do this in way that nothing else does. Bondage helps me take this powerful broad beam of light and hone it into a fine laser that I can direct.

Trusting Alex didn't happen immediately. Like most people, I really have to get to know someone before I dare to be at all vulnerable. But now when I work with Alex, I find myself in a place of absolute trust, and somehow, learning to allow myself to be that vulnerable has allowed me to become calm and redirect my big energy.

The year I started working with Alex was a big year; a lot of things happened. My whole life changed. My family, my work, my relationship, my sexuality—it's all different now. That year my youngest brother died very suddenly of a heart attack. That was huge. We were very close. He was only forty-one. You know, when you lose a family member, the family structure changes and it throws everyone off. His wife and young daughter were with him when he died. I can't even imagine what that was like. There was a tremendous load put on everyone. My parents lost their youngest child! It all impacted me greatly. I'm very close to my family; they're great people. So I did a lot of reaching out, supporting and dealing with emotions. Then shortly after my brother's death, my father had a stroke. He's recovering well, but my family has had a really tough time with it all. We've all had a tough time.

In another part of my world, I was granted two huge public art commissions. I'm a sculptress. The commissions were very exciting and equally startling. With the work came a great deal of anxiety. You know, when someone says they think you're really good at what you do, you have to show up and really be that good. You have to believe in yourself and demonstrate that you are worthy, and you have to be able to focus a tremendous amount of energy to be that good.

To top it all off, I had ended a seven-year relationship. That was very tough, but ultimately, also very good. It was a wonderful relationship. We both learned so much from it. It was a great opening for us, and I am grateful that we stuck it out and did our work. I learned a lot about myself, about communicating, about being in relationship, about commitment and about learning to trust.

Four years into our relationship, we took a big chance and decided to open our relationship up. Even at the time, I had serious doubts about the wisdom of that decision. Changing the dynamics of our relationship in that way—shifting from one modality (monogamy) to another (non-monogamy)—brought about tremendous issues of trust, fear and jealousy. My hope was that my partner would be able to get involved with someone else and still come back to me. It was important to me that the outside relationships not deplete, diminish or eclipse our relationship, but that they actually bring something wonderful that would feed our relationship. In the end, that didn't happen.

Initially we experienced a wonderful sexual awakening; an excitement of sexuality. We shared that for a while, but then it became very difficult for us. Ultimately, my partner met someone that she wanted to marry and have children with. So my intuition about polyamory was pretty accurate. It's very risky business. But then love is risky; in fact, people fall in love outside of declared monogamous relations all the time. The heart doesn't always follow the rules.

> *...when someone says they think you're really good at what you do, you have to show up and really be that good.*

It seems like there is always something positive to be learned from a difficult situation. Ultimately, what came out of this moment in time was a new sense of the scope of the erotic playing field. It was big. So I allowed myself to ask, "What do I really want? What feeds me and where do I choose to explore beyond the edges of convention?" I wrestled with my desire to explore Sadomasochism for quite a while. It both thrilled me and scared me. Then I woke up one morning and realized that desire had won the battle. I was going to explore. The thought was like a drug. It was something that imbued me with the most excitement I've ever felt in my body. There was something deeply empowering when I finally allowed myself to accept and honor my desires. My inner world began to shift.

> *It's so ironic that placing myself in the role of submission allows me to walk out into the world more powerful than I have ever been able to be in my life.*

So many positive transformations have happened as a result of following that longing. From the moment I gave myself permission to explore, I began to experience a deep release of tension and with that, a release of creative energy. That release grows stronger and stronger with every bondage experience. I also experience a greater sense of personal power with each session. It's so ironic that placing myself in the role of submission allows me to walk out into the world more powerful than I have ever been able to be in my life. I used to have a tendency to be very shy. I would have a really difficult time when I had to meet with art committees to present my work. I would get extremely insecure and tongue-tied, but now, when I talk about my work, I get very passionate. Now, I walk into a committee and I am amazed at how well I can articulate the meaning of my work and how I approach it.

Honoring my desire was how I took an irreversible leap into my personal power. I think that the bottom line is *authenticity*. That's the important thing. I remember how it was when I was getting ready to go for my interview with a large public arts commission. That was really the big league. I felt like all my life I had been playing on the farm team and I was finally being called up. I really didn't think I was going to get the commission, but I still wanted to go to the interview and give it my best shot. So before my interview, I went down to this small lake in Seattle and I meditated. As I sat there, the words that kept coming into my mind like a mantra were, "Be yourself." I knew that the only thing I could do was to go into that meeting and be myself. Being myself was the best thing I could give them. I walked in, and I was myself. I didn't have a slide carousel and neither did they, so I just introduced my work in a very casual way. We joked, and I went off on tangents, and I knew when I walked out of the meeting that I had captivated every one of them. I knew that I had interviewed better than ever before, and that the commission was mine. I knew that I was myself. I was Julie Berger.

Long before "holistic" became part of the mainstream vocabulary, Dr. Rudolph Ballentine, author of Radical Healing, *was already weaving Tantra, Ayurvedic medicine, homeopathy, nutrition and yoga into an integrated approach to natural healing. Holistic describes Rudy perfectly. He is a healer, author, psychiatrist, father, Tantra teacher, sacred intimate and visionary. His style is quiet, inquisitive and unassuming. Rudy's modest wisdom and clear reasoning make him the consummate teacher. Even as he was working to find the right words to articulate less than fully birthed ideas, he was giving valuable lessons. After an hour and a half interview with Rudy, I felt as if I had been given the keys to unlock some universal truths. Recently, Rudy has turned his attention toward mentoring those who are ready to look, in greater depth, at their erotic connections with others and explore sexuality as a spiritual path. I left our conversation changed and felt better equipped for life.*

Rudolph Ballentine, MD

I never really intended to be a doctor. That was not my goal. My goal was to understand what makes people tick. In the 1950s, the prevailing opinion seemed to be that psychology held the answer, which is why I majored in psychology and planned to get a PhD in that field. Then someone said to me, "Well, if you do that, you'll just end up taking orders from a psychiatrist." I wasn't interested in taking orders from anybody, so I went to medical school where I chose psychiatry as my specialty. During the course of my training, I did a general medicine internship in Panama, which gave me a taste of what it really means to be a healer — to really help someone improve the quality of their life. To my surprise, that aspect of medicine, one that I thought I really wasn't interested in, opened my heart. Seeing people suffering and feeling that I could do something that would really make a difference touched something deep in me. I hadn't known either of those things. I hadn't known that people were suffering so, and I didn't know I could actually make a difference!

During my time there, one of the women who came to me for help was from a remote village, where she was a nurse and the only healer for many miles around. People would carry patients for days to be treated by her in that wild place. She taught me a lesson in how back-to-basics, simple, compassionate medicine could make a significant difference. By helping her back to wellness, I knew that many, many people were able to continue to have access to good medical care.

When I saw that the medications used to treat mental illness often forced the mental suffering back into the physical body, I realized that a body/mind approach to healing was needed.

I completed my residency in psychiatry but eventually become disillusioned with the use of medications in treating mental illness.

My heart had been struck by the physical suffering I witnessed in Panama. When I saw that the medications used to treat mental illness often forced the mental suffering back into the physical body, I realized that a body/mind approach to healing was needed. I knew there had to be some deeper, broader, more encompassing perspective. I gravitated toward analysis and psychoanalytic psychotherapy, but that still seemed a little constricted to me. I began searching for something I would later come to think of as "spiritual."

During my residency, I was working in New Orleans where I helped set up a free clinic for street kids. There, I learned about spiritual traditions from the East and Native American traditions. At the same time, I was reading Carlos Castañeda, and these things began to open my mind. I discovered other aspects of both healing and expanding consciousness, and that's when I decided I had to go to India. This was 1972 or 1973. I went alone, which was a big step for me.

In India, I met Swami Rama who became my teacher. He taught me about yoga, homeopathy, Ayurveda and Tantra, though I didn't recognize the teachings as Tantric at the time. Swami Rama found me a partner, got me married, got me through that experience, and after twelve years, got me unmarried. I have four children from that marriage that I am very devoted to. I spent twenty years working very closely with Swami Rama, under his supervision and guidance. Some of that time I spent in India, but most of the time I lived in the U.S., working and living at the Himalayan Institute which he established. The Institute is a national and international network of centers that teach the integration of mind and body healing in a sophisticated approach, which is based on the traditions of Indian philosophy and Tantra.

One of the biggest changes in my life began in 1992 when I went to Colombia, South America, to lead an intensive on holistic medicine. Being in that culture and teaching in that language was a very exciting experience for me. I felt like a different person, more embodied and a lot more erotically alive. I don't know quite why, but there is something about Latin America that gives me more permission to be in my body. I probably would not have come back to the U.S. at all had it not been for my four kids. I loved it so!

When I did come back, I got very sick. Actually I felt like I got sick as I was leaving Columbia. People around me were saying things like, "Oh, you must have picked up a parasite." But there was never any evidence of that. What I felt was that I picked up a vision or a glimpse of a different way of living that I didn't want to leave. I got seriously sick. I couldn't sleep. I couldn't eat. I couldn't take three breaths without coughing. Tests didn't show any reason for it, but I was just fading away. One of the doctors that I had trained came and taped my ribs, which were snapping when I coughed because I had become so fragile. I even reacted to the tape so much that when she took it off, my whole chest had become raw and oozing. I felt like Job! I was really a mess.

My family finally brought me back to my little cottage in Pennsylvania where I sat and listened to people whispering that they thought I was dying. I thought I was dying. I realized the gravity of the situation, because I had begun to think about dying in an optimistic way. I was enough of a physician to know that if I continued in that direction, I would reach a point of no return. I knew that I'd better damn well be sure that dying was what I really wanted to do.

I started reflecting on the important parts of my life. My kids, though they spent a lot of time with me, were in good hands with my ex-wife, and I knew that she had the resources to take care of them. I had written books and devoted twenty years to the Himalayan Institute, so I thought that it was not an unreasonable or inappropriate time for me to die. People would say, "Well, he did wonderful work, lived a good life, etc." But I was at a loss as to how to determine if this was really my time to go. I had plenty of time to contemplate, because I was just sitting there in my cabin with nothing to do but cough and look out the window. So I thought to myself, "You're smart; you can invent some way to determine whether it's your time to die."

Then I thought up a simple experiential test in which I would think of things and see how I felt in my body. I thought of work at the Himalayan Institute and my whole body wilted. That evidence was clear. I wasn't going to stay on this planet for the Institute. I thought of my children and felt a deep sadness, but I didn't feel my life energy come back. I couldn't live just for them. I'm not proud to say that, but that was true. Then I thought about my sexuality and I thought about exploring the homosexual parts of myself that had been ignored. I felt an upsurge in energy. Just opening to the possibility of this untapped energy was powerfully healing. I felt myself sitting up straighter, and I thought, "Okay, maybe that's what you can live for. Maybe you can stay alive to do that!" I suppose it took being on that threshold of death to bring out something so thoroughly, so deeply buried in me. Death's imminence was very liberating. I realized that I had shut the door on that part of my life, that I had unfinished, unresolved business. I realized that my life was not yet complete. Maybe I felt a deep aversion to leaving something unfinished. Maybe it was curiosity, but whatever it was, it was enough to bring the will to live back into my body. Right there I made a decision to stay alive and investigate this sexual or erotic energy.

Then, having made the decision, I realized that I had no idea how do that! Having no clue where to begin, I fumbled around for the next two or three years. My fumbling was compounded by the fact that I was still president of the Himalayan Institute and everyone, including me, had the idea that my work, for life, was there. I had been at the Institute from its inception, and I was written in as its Acharya, which means I was the president and spiritual head of the organization. When I declared that I was leaving, it caused some serious upset. I had to disentangle myself from that work bit by bit, and every time I gave in to someone else's expectations, I would start coughing again. Even today, if I start to endeavor in the wrong direction, I'll start to cough. I've become very grateful for that cough.

Finally, I was able to withdraw from the Institute, but then I had to figure out how to go about exploring sexuality and the erotic energy that is provoked or created by sexual attraction. I wanted to discover where erotic energy comes from, what it is about, how it works, how I could get under it and use it in ways beyond relationship. What I found in the world of same sex unions was a crushing, internalized homophobia, creating huge guilt-ridden, impulsive connections, and not much sense of freedom to explore with honest consciousness. I didn't know where to go or who to talk to, so I decided to go to men who advertised erotic massage in the newspaper. I told each of these men that I wanted to just feel and begin to understand the erotic energy—that I wasn't there just to get off! Most of them looked at me as if to say, "You're nuts! That's what people come to me for, to get off!"

Then I happened upon another man, a man named Christopher who was a retired naval officer. I made my usual request, and braced for the usual response, but he said, "Well, great! That's what I do. That's always the way I do it." I was taken by surprise. I asked him where he had learned that, and he told me about The Body Electric School. Of course I wanted to know more. Christopher handed me a brochure when I left. I went home and promptly put it in a drawer. Then, each day, for many days, I pulled the brochure out of the drawer and looked at it with a mixture of dread and intrigue. I was terrified by my own internalized homophobia, but I finally got enough courage and went to an introductory event in Washington, DC.

During my entire drive from New York, I listened to Louise Hay on tape telling me over and over, "You're okay, you're okay." I kept playing the tape the whole time, because I was really in a panic. I don't think I would have gotten to the event without Louise. When I arrived, I was surprised by how warm, open-hearted and normal everyone was, but I still wasn't

That simple exercise of connecting my heart with my sexual energy was huge and powerful.

convinced I belonged there. I was thinking, "Well, they're all queer and I'm not!" I felt completely out of place, and I thought, "I should just go home." But for some reason, I felt compelled to stay and I'm really glad I did.

The next morning changed everything for me. We did a simple exercise that I found very transformative. We paired off and each of us stood naked in front of another man. Then each man put a hand on the other's heart. That simple exercise of connecting my heart with my sexual energy was huge and powerful. The whole weekend was life changing for many reasons. For one, I knew the techniques and attitude of Tantra, but I didn't have a container or arena for erotic exploration. This weekend provided that for me. Within a year, I had done five Body Electric events — most of the curriculum, including the Sacred Intimate Training, which was a wonderful experience for me. I loved it all and learned so much.

I then began to assist with some of the workshops. It was at one of these events that Collin Brown came up to me and said, "I'm realizing that you have so much to offer. I'd like for you to come and teach a Tantra workshop for Body Electric." I burst into tears. In that moment, I realized that this was exactly what I had been living for. This was what I stayed on this earth to do, and I'd been waiting for the chance. So I said, "Disregard the tears. I really want to do it."

Somewhere along the way of teaching Tantra, I realized that a major part of what I'm called to do is support a redefinition of sexuality and what it offers us, or — to use a Buddhist expression — to ask "What is the 'right use' of sexuality?" Our culture holds a certain set of prejudices about sexuality that mostly have to do with religious taboos and economic exploitation. I recognize that there is a certain period of life, the time of child bearing and rearing, where it really makes sense for sexuality to function in a socially regulated fashion. You need to create a household that has stability. After those years, or for people who choose not to have children, it's possible to move into a different attitude about the potentials and possibilities of sexuality.

At the core of this other kind of attitude is a realm for us to explore where we can mine our sexuality for the power, wisdom and healing it holds. It's also a place where you can uncover your unhealed pieces so that you can bring them into consciousness and heal them. Healing always involves reintegrating a part of the self that was separate, unconscious, cut off or buried. This is all the same project. You go in and discover the things that you've pushed down into your sexuality, the things that are being expressed through your sexual life, and when you bring those pieces into consciousness, a release and a healing takes place. Then, the energy that was tied up in that bit of sexuality becomes available for all the other aspects of life — other erotic experiences, creative pursuits or to activate other channels of energy.

> *Healing always involves reintegrating a part of the self that was separate, unconscious, cut off or buried.*

The prevailing attitude in our culture is fraught with fears that inhibit us and make it illegitimate to explore the world of our sexuality. As a consequence, we aren't doing it in the free, open and productive way that we could. That's a huge problem. As a psychiatrist, healer and teacher of Tantra, I believe sexuality is commonly the place where we dump our unexamined neurotic, and even psychotic, stuff. The aspects of ourselves that are totally crazy, or aspects that we are simply not willing to look at, often get channeled through and acted out in the world through our sexuality, because that's a place where nobody will mess with it. Psychotherapists like to say that once something is "sexualized" (relegated to the area of sexuality), it's untreatable. Once something gets encoded into sexual identity or sexual patterns, it's hard to deal with, because we can't go there. It's off limits, taboo — a psychotherapist could end up in court and lose his or her license. A sacred intimate or sacred prostitute, on the other hand, can work directly with a sexual behavior, bringing consciousness to that behavior.

Psychotherapists like to say that once something is "sexualized" …it's untreatable.

Any kind of unresolved primitive stuff can be channeled through the sexuality. An example would be that someone might have issues about self-confidence. They go to great lengths to ensure that they are sexually attractive. Then each time that attractiveness gets reinforced they feel confident, but that confidence must constantly be reinforced. The underlying reasons for their core lack of confidence may never be addressed, because their sexuality cannot be addressed.

We have violent forces, churches, laws, political structures, teachers and families admonishing us, "Don't go there. Don't you dare look into your sexuality." I believe that the biggest impediment to exploring sexuality freely is overwhelming homophobia, especially for men, because when you get in there, you can't tell where the exploration is going to go. It has to be free to go wherever it goes. I'm totally convinced that when men explore their sexuality freely, most men—not just some men, but most men—are going to find some attraction to people of their own sex. I'm also totally convinced that that will never be the whole of who they are. I'm convinced that when they explore the homoerotic part of themselves, they're much more able to explore, in a genuine way, their connection with the opposite sex.

Perhaps the most important personal and global issues that lie locked in our sexuality are issues about gender and power which are central to the planetary crisis that we're facing. We have a lot of confusion and misconception about the nature of power. What's missing is the understanding of feminine power and the proper use of the masculine. In the Tantric tradition—and I believe this to be true—energetic, creative, erotic, active power is an attribute of the feminine, not the masculine. That is not to say that this power is an attribute found only in women. It is simply to say the active power in everyone is feminine. Feelings of frustration, anger, and disempowerment arise in men who do not own their feminine power, and this is why we are living in such a destructive time. The nature of the true masculine gift is consciousness—a consciousness with a

> *As long as the feminine is disempowered, the world will be in a state of rage.*

capacity to penetrate, to plumb the depths of complex situations and to direct energy. If we use this consciousness properly, instead of reacting with violence in a crisis, we can bring understanding, healing and peace to the event. Coming to grips with this paradox and this blindness about the nature of power is crucial. This blindness is the linchpin that holds together our global madness. As long as the feminine is disempowered, the world will be in a state of rage.

Tantric work is about recognizing that the feminine and masculine exist in each person. It is about the integration or inner marriage of the two. One meaning of Tantra is weaving—in this case, the weaving is between the masculine and feminine in each of us. The weaving is also between our inner struggle and the planetary struggle. This is so important, because it brings the war and the way to peace home, home to our inner world where we do have the capacity to make changes. We must bring the war home. We cannot sustain the status quo, the global madness. We have to create tranquility and peace inside of each one of us. Everybody's got to do that. We are each and every one the microcosm of the macrocosm, the macrocosmic global madness. If the power of the feminine is understood, embraced and set free, we will see radical changes.

> *Love means that you care so much about another that your deepest desire is to see them fully blossom into just who they naturally are.*

The structure of the world as we know it cannot stand, for it is based on a paradigm in which power is confused with force and violence. We need a radically different paradigm that honors the spontaneous creative energy of the feminine. An appropriate trust in "Her" is exactly what this planet needs. This feminine power is a pure expression of love, and when it emerges, it shatters what is superfluous, confusing, and stifling to our authentic expression. In the Tantric tradition, love is about caring for others enough to allow them to be truly who they are. Love means that you care so much about another that your deepest desire is to see them fully blossom into just who they naturally are. Love does not demand or attach. Operating within this paradigm would not support invading another country with the intention of obliterating their culture so as to make them into something that serves one's own needs. That's force, not power.

What we perceive as security—a terribly false security given the current state of the world—will be jeopardized by the unleashing of the feminine power. This is radical! It will bring the whole system down, so it's understandable that we feel terrified. Because of that, anything that is feminine needs to be ridiculed and discredited. The masculine is terrified of the feminine, because if she ever gets loose, she will destroy his world. His pseudo power will be exposed as the fraud that it is, and it will be shattered. Homophobia is a kind of fear of the feminine, because we are afraid of the feminine within and without. When I say "we," I mean both men and women, because we are all bisexual in the sense that we are all masculine and feminine internally. We all have this frustrated, raging, impotent masculine inside of us, having a tantrum. In men, it is much more obvious. In men it is almost a caricature, but women, too, have a masculine.

Women, too, participate in the demeaning of the feminine. We're all dealing with that.

When the true feminine power, the creative power, comes forth, she will destroy the economic systems, the political systems and the religious systems—everything we have constructed. This feminine, this part of me, will destroy my world, and thank God, because so much of the world needs to be destroyed. Our world is in a terrible state. Something needs to collapse so that something better can be built. My plea is for bringing humanity back to the earth by recognizing the importance of exploring our embodiment, our earthiness, and by honoring the fullness of human nature.

Rudolph Ballentine, MD

Years before I experienced the joy of Sheri's teaching, I had heard about her great classes on female anatomy. It was rumored that Sheri's knowledge about women's anatomy was encyclopedic. The rumor was not an exaggeration. Several years ago I joined Sheri and about thirty other women for a one-day workshop — time and a little money extremely well spent. She is smart, playful, powerful, funny and compassionate as she shares her infectious joy about the wonders of a woman's body. Sheri knows that knowledge is power and power is joy. She says it, she teaches it and she embodies it. Wouldn't it be wonderful if Sheri's teaching were part of every middle school and high school health curriculum? I can dream!

PHOTO CREDIT: MARGARET SINGER

Sheri Winston, CNM

You might say that my career as a teacher of holistic sexuality began when I was nine. My beloved cat, Misty, woke me one night as she was about to give birth. I crawled under the bed and stayed with her as she delivered her beautiful kittens and I was with her all the way as she raised them. Misty was my first midwife client and my teacher on how to be a good mom. She was so special—how she cared for her kittens, how she nursed them. She showed me what breast feeding should look like—blissed-out, divine union.

I am very blessed. I grew up in a relatively sexually healthy household. I grew up with parents who had a great sex life, and I didn't grow up with a lot of religious baggage about sex and bodies. When I was about twelve, my mother gave me a copy of the very first edition of *Our Bodies Ourselves*; originally called the *Boston Women's Health Book Collective*, written by twelve Boston feminist activists and first published in 1973. I consider that to be a great privilege — to have been given a book like that at that age. I've also never experienced any kind of sexual abuse or aggression. Sometimes I think I must have had a guardian angel looking out for me, but it's sad that I consider these things a privilege rather than the norm. Still, no one escapes the culture entirely. Even though I grew up in a really healthy home environment, I still had to deal with cultural stuff like how "good girls" are supposed to act and what "sexy women" are supposed to look like. Everybody's got stuff.

Birthing will teach you about women's nature and women's power in a way that almost nothing else can.

My first career ambition was to be an artist, but it didn't take long before I realized that being an artist wasn't going to be a great way to make a living. So, at the age of twenty, I decided to become a massage therapist. At that point I knew I was going on to some other type of healing work, but it wasn't clear what that was going to be. I was thinking about midwifery, but I was also thinking about medical school. Then I got to go to a home birth and that pretty much cinched the deal. That became my calling. I became a childbirth educator—a *Doula*—and an apprentice midwife. In order to legally practice midwifery in New York State, you have to have a bachelor's degree in nursing; for that reason alone, I put myself through nursing school. I worked with homebirth midwives for some time. Then, in 1990, I went to midwifery school and got my CNM (Certified Nurse Midwife) degree, which included gynecology. Midwifery is some of the most amazing work I could ever think of doing. I was so lucky to fall into the world of birth—particularly midwife-attended home birth. Birthing will teach you about women's nature and women's power in a way that almost nothing else can.

I'm so blessed and so grateful that I got to attend all of those miraculous births, but now, as I get older, my mission gets bigger. The calling has expanded from a very intimate mission to quite literally wanting to change the world—wanting to transform our culture, our planet, through sexuality. When I stopped catching babies and started teaching sexuality, I didn't change paths—I went deeper and wider into the same mystery.

In 1999, after twenty years and over seven hundred births, I grew really frustrated. I hit burnout status. The hours, the responsibility, and the politics of fighting the fight for healthier, happier, more empowered birth experiences got to me, so I took a break from midwifery and started practicing gynecology. If, when I was in my twenties, you had asked, "Are women going to have less intervention, fewer Cesarean sections and better birth experiences?" I would have said, "Yes, everything is going to be better in ten years, and in twenty years, it's going to be great!" But by the time I had turned forty, it had become worse than ever. Cesarean rates were higher than ever.

More women were having epidurals, missing the full birth experience, and fewer women were breast feeding. What I realized is that we are never going to be able to heal birth in our culture until we heal sex. If we don't understand and acknowledge that birth is a sexual process, how can we help women have amazing and powerful births? That's not going to change until we understand our sexuality. We need to understand what birth is and what it can be. We need to know where the power lies; how we can we can access it and utilize it for good and for health. When we get that piece, so much will change.

> *If we don't understand and acknowledge that birth is a sexual process, how can we help women have amazing and powerful births?*

Our current cultural understanding about sex is shallow, fear-based, and laden with shame. Our understanding is limited by a domination model, which is based on the premise of getting something and losing something. It also includes the idea that your present experience of your sexuality is what you're stuck with. And if that sexuality isn't working for you, then there must be something wrong with you. In my model of sexuality, what I call "Wholistic Sexuality," things are different. First, I believe our sexuality starts with ourselves; it's about connection, but about connection with our own life energy. Sex makes life—life makes sex. We wouldn't be here if our parents didn't have sex. It's one of the two most primal forces on the planet—personal survival and reproduction. So, whether or not you choose to actually reproduce, your sexuality connects you to all of life on the planet. It's not what we do, it's who we are.

Sexuality is a combination of mind, heart, body, spirit—everything. It's also a combination of our hardware and software. The hardware—what we came equipped with—is our evolutionary template. But because we're human, we're wired with cultural software as well. When we start to understand how much of our sexuality is *learned*, it shifts any sense of being broken or defective. Once we understand that sex is learnable and realize that we can get rid of old, dysfunctional programming, we can begin to import new programming. We become aware of the limitations of the current software and thus can embrace new possibilities. These are learnable skills and once learned it's possible to start seeing sex as a way of connecting—not giving, not getting, not taking, but simply connecting. We can also learn that sex is not about the way you look. You don't have to be twenty years old, a size two, and look like a model in order to have amazing sex. Sexy is about who you are.

> *Sexuality is a combination of mind, heart, body, spirit— everything. It's also a combination of our hardware and software.*

The place to start learning how to have amazing sex is with your self. There is no right way, no wrong way. It's all about what works for you, so start thinking about your sexual experience as an experiment. Notice what works, what you like, what you don't like, and practice. Like anything, if you want to get better at something, practice.

I like to use musical analogies; everyone is born with some musical ability, but whether you learn to play an instrument well or not is up to you. Most of us are just kind of messing around with the keys. We've learned to play some simple tunes, but nobody ever sat down with us and said, "Hey, here's your instrument and it has all these cool parts and they work together like this. You can play it like this; you can play it like that. You can play solo or you can play a duet. You can even play with a band!" Learning to play your instrument well is about learning technique, and having amazing sex is like creating great musical improvisation.

Imagine that you've been playing the piano for many years, all the while thinking that there were twenty-two keys. To your delight, you find out that there are not only eighty-eight keys, but also two foot pedals! And then, even more exciting, you find out that you have this beautifully integrated system that includes reproduction, pleasure and emotional bonding—a trio. These are not three separate systems. They are interlocking and overlapping, and there is an owner's manual. If you understand the system, you can learn to operate it better whether you're the owner/operator or a privileged visitor.

> *...women have as much erectile tissue as men!*

One common attitude about sex is that once we reach a certain point, once we know certain things that work well for us, we're done learning. But, like virtuoso musicians, we're never done learning. If you love to play the guitar, you're always asking, "What else can I do with my guitar?" If you're bored or sex has become a chore, maybe it's because you've stopped learning. Maybe you're playing the same old tune over and over again?

Most women know very little about their anatomy and how it functions. Surprisingly, even most health care providers don't understand the entire female anatomy. For instance: women have as much erectile tissue as men! Erectile tissue is the fabulous expandable tissue that gives the penis its amazing ability to go from small and soft to big and hard. Women have just as much of that expandable, engorgeable, sensitive tissue as men do. The difference is that it lies in a network of structures, and most women don't know where all of those structures are located. Picture the head of the clitoris — that is a part we all know about. The head of the clitoris is part of a three-part structure. The clitoris also has a shaft which is underneath the hood and two legs like a wishbone that extend down on either side. We have another pair of structures called vestibular bulbs. These are shaped like commas. The bottom of this structure wraps around the opening of the vagina, underneath the labia, and the top connects to the shaft of the clitoris. These vestibular bulbs can get quite big and puffy and they are part of what makes it feel good to have something inside the vaginal opening. There's also the structure called the G-spot, though I really don't care for that name. Grafenberg, after whom it's named, doesn't have one, and it's not really a spot. The so-called G-spot is really a tube of erectile tissue that surrounds the urethra, so I prefer to call it the urethral sponge. The way to access the urethral sponge is through and up above the roof of the vagina. All of this erectile tissue is more obvious and easier to find when a woman is aroused, and may be irritated if touched before arousal.

There's also erectile tissue on the floor of the vagina, between the vagina and anal canal. So, that whole network of structures is, on average, equivalent to the erectile tissue a man has in his penis. It's all connected, but not a singular unit like the penis. Women can be aroused and become orgasmic with just part of the network activated; that is what most of us experience. We're aware of the head of the clitoris and maybe the shaft, but for the best arousal and best orgasm, you really want to get all of the structures activated.

The uterus is also a foundational player in the process of arousal and orgasm. The uterus moves up and forward during arousal, and during orgasm it bounces up and down, contributing a significant component of the orgasmic sensation. It's really important for women to know this, since our medical model holds that once you're done having babies, you don't really need your uterus. As a consequence, we have an insanely high rate of unnecessary hysterectomies. If women (and the people who love them) knew more about the marvelous complexity of their body's arousal, they could make better-informed choices.

Arousal and orgasm are extremely healthy in many ways. Orgasms release endorphins, natural pleasure-enhancing, pain-killing chemicals. Orgasms stimulate our immune systems to work better. You also get the benefits of aerobic exercise—you breathe and oxygenate. Arousal and orgasms help our moods—help us be happy. I think that all the anti-depressant and anti-anxiety medications that people are taking could be seriously reduced if people went on a regular program of frequent and powerful orgasms. If orgasms weren't sex-related, health care providers would be telling everyone to have lots of them. If you're partnered, sharing pleasure and orgasm with that partner can be the glue and the lubricant of a long-term, healthy relationship.

Orgasm is a birthright. We're born ecstatic (if we have a great birth experience). To have access to that pleasure and euphoria and ecstasy is very important. People who are orgasm-challenged can feel bad, sad, ripped-off and broken. Not only is orgasm important for the experience itself, because it's pleasurable and health-enhancing, but I think it's also key in feeling like a whole human being—to have the same experience others are having.

Why do I care so much? Why am I dedicating myself to teaching Wholistic Sexuality? This is what I'm here to do. I'm so privileged to have the upbringing, education, experiences, friends and teachers that enable me to see these connections—to see how this all fits

...all the anti-depressant and anti-anxiety medications that people are taking could be seriously reduced if people went on a regular program of frequent and powerful orgasms.

together. If I didn't share this, it would be wrong. It would be as if someone had brought me a feast for a hundred people and I just kept it all for myself. I think I've always been a teacher—no matter what I was doing. When I was a massage therapist, I taught massage classes. Then I taught childbirth classes, classes on breastfeeding, infant massage, vaginal ecology and alternative women's health. Teaching is where the juice is for me. I love empowering other people—love seeing the light go on in their eyes when they really get something. I get complete and utter joy from being an agent for that. I think the world would be a better place if people had more knowledge about how their bodies operate. If I can help people have better sex, be healthier and happier, be more knowledgeable and feel better about themselves, that's really good—good for the planet. It's not only about individuals—it's global.

I believe that all violence is actually distorted sexual energy. The sexual energy within us is a powerful force and it's going to express itself. It's going to get out somehow. It's our choice whether it gets expressed as positive energy in the form of connection, pleasure, joy and love, or if it gets repressed, distorted and comes out violently. I do not believe that someone can have amazing, ecstatic, blissful sexual joy and then be violent. It just doesn't add up. So, I look at my work as part of the consciousness shift that has to occur if human beings are going to find their way to creating a more gentle, more kind world. The microcosm of our personal relationship with our sexuality impacts the macrocosm of the world we live in. When enough people connect to their own pleasure and ecstasy, the shift away from violence will happen.

It's not hard to find examples of how denying pleasurable connection with other beings leads to unhappy, unhealthy, aggressive people. In my years as a midwife I saw over and over how babies, born via natural birth, in a loving, affectionate environment, came

> *I believe that all violence is actually distorted sexual energy.*

out peaceful and ecstatic—all babies. But most of us did not have that loving, natural birth. Most of us had hospital births that involved a lot of fear and trauma, and not enough touch.

We can also look at the dominant influences in our own history. Here in the United States, we are dealing with a couple thousand years of dominant Christian culture which, especially over the last thousand years, has been very sex- and pleasure-negative. Sexually repressive cultures maintain an effective hierarchy. Power is the motivation. People at the top of the hierarchy need to dominate, and sexual repression is a very effective strategy for achieving that. Sex-negative cultures, bound by rigid laws, are also women-negative cultures. The two always go together. When you have egalitarian cultures where both genders (or all genders) are revered and have equal, if not identical power, you find sex-positive cultures.

So (tongue in cheek), I'm trying to change the world one orgasm at a time! I travel a lot—teaching—everything from hour-long classes to week-long retreats. I teach women, men, singles, partners and people of all orientations and inclinations. There are classes for teens and parents of teens. Occasionally I do some professional training and speak at conferences. My classes range from anatomy lectures to workshops which build skills for enhancing sexual experiences by using breath, sound, movement and imagination. I'm also developing an online curriculum—webinars, DVDs and ebooks. The idea is to make this knowledge accessible to people in the comfort and privacy of their homes.

Then there's my book, *Women's Anatomy of Arousal: Secret Maps to Buried Pleasure* which won the Book of the Year award from

AASECT, the American Association of Sex Educators, Counselors and Therapists. That felt really validating. The first part of the book looks at models and mental constructs that we have about sexuality. The heart (or crotch) of my book is a tour of women's anatomy—complete with illustrations. (My art training finally paid off!) The book describes how you can use the information to become a sexual virtuoso—with yourself or with a partner, if you choose. Dr. Christian Northrop called this "the most important book about sex," saying that every woman, their partners and their health care providers need to read this book.

When I teach, the biggest "a-ha" moments come when a woman realizes she already has all the power tools she needs inside. Women who have never had an orgasm, or feel orgasm-challenged—a substantial number of women—believe that they're broken, that there's something wrong with them. Then they come to a class. They learn to breath, move and visualize, and suddenly it becomes so clear—they get how it all connects. They begin to understand their sexual potential. They see a personal treasure map, and once they know the path they can follow it whenever they choose. It might take practice to become really adept, but what an awakening!

The power tools I'm referring to tend to be found in four buckets. There is a bucket full of tools for the mind, one for the body, one for the heart and one for the spirit. They're not really separate; they overlap, but to simplify, think of it this way: the body tools include things like the breath, sound, touch, movement, smell and taste. Then there are the tools of the mind—awareness, intention, attention and imagination. We have tools of the heart—the skills of loving. Heart skills teach you to stay open, to have courage, to transform fear with love and to distinguish healthy fear from unhealthy fear. We use the tools of the spirit to create altars and to make sacred space and rituals for sex. Different people will be attracted to different tool buckets. Some people will be very attracted to the tools of the spirit, but for others it's not such a draw. It's important to remember that there's no right way to use these tools—there's only what works for you. Your job is to run experiments in your own little laboratory and find out what works.

Last year, during the opening circle on the Sunday morning of a weekend retreat, one of the women began to talk about the sex she'd had with her husband the night before. She revealed that she had experienced the first orgasm of her life—the first! In fact, she'd had several! She looked so different—transformed from the woman who had walked in two days before. She was a very attractive woman and because of our models, you would assume that she probably had great sex—but you'd be wrong. Here she was revealing that, until that night, she had never had an orgasmic experience. She and her husband were just glowing and almost everyone there was tearing up—it was really emotional.

At another workshop, a sixty-three-year-old woman burst out in tears. I gently asked her what was going on and she revealed that in the past year of her life, between sixty-two and sixty-three, she'd had the first three orgasms of her life. She said she was determined not to live the rest of her life without knowing how to have an orgasm whenever she wanted to. She's been having partner sex since she was twenty and she was grieving the interim decades of not knowing, not having that experience. She was grieving how it affected her life and her relationships. Why had no one ever told her about this? Why did she have to wait until she was sixty-three to learn about her own body and have orgasmic experiences?

Both of these stories are cultural extremes, but they illustrate the need for and the gift of erotic education. We need to teach more. We should be learning about our bodies, starting as children. We should all have a lifetime of this. Thousands of years of sex-negative culture and the shame and fear of our history are what we're overcoming. We've come a long way—really. When I was twelve, *Our Bodies Ourselves* was revolutionary. It was one of the few books out there with any depth of information for women. Now there are many books out that have pieces of information for us.

We're on the path, but we have a lot to do. I think of the human species as being a very young species. We're in that ridiculous adolescent stage where we have a lot of power, but we don't quite know what to do with it. We stumble around, driven by our urges, yet failing to foresee the consequences of our behavior. Still, we are making progress.

Sheri Winston, CNM

If you have a problem believing that bondage and sadism can be tools of love and healing, you are not alone. Until I met Singing Deer, I also had a hard time plugging that idea into my circuitry. Singing Deer does not fit into the stereotypical image of a dominatrix. She's compassionate, soft, seductive, pretty, and feminine. She is also powerful and courageous. Whenever I'm with Singing Deer, I feel that I really matter. She is uniquely present and caring. In her easy Southern speech, she refers to "spirit" with a sureness and familiarity few have. It's clear that this is the source of her strength.

Singing Deer

People get confused when they hear my name, Singing Deer. They wonder, "What kind of a name is that for a Mistress?" But my name says something about my nature. Deer medicine is strength through gentleness. My name offers people a chance to expand their concept of who I am and what I might offer. Some people may call me a dominatrix or a pro domme, but I don't identify with that. Those labels are only useful to describe a very narrow picture of what I offer.

For as long as I can remember I've been very sensual, nurturing and very adventuresome, so it's no surprise that I was drawn to sacred intimate work. I had my first experience at nineteen. I didn't know what to make of it, and I didn't have any mentors at that time, but I kept being drawn back to the idea of working with erotic energy. So I sought out some inspiring teachers to help me along the way. I looked to the teachings of Margo Anand to learn about Tantra and sex magic. I've also learned from the writings of Thich Nhat Hanh and Joseph Campbell, but Alex Jade, Selah Martha and Emaya have been my most valuable teachers. (See Alex Jade's and Emaya's stories elsewhere in this collection.) When I'm around them, I become a sponge soaking up the pearls of wisdom that drop from their mouths. Something that I find so rare and remarkable in these women is that they don't hold themselves above those who are learning from them. They're just very human, humble and vulnerable, which are qualities essential to sacred intimate work. Without those qualities, big mistakes can be made.

When I decided to become a sacred intimate, I thought I would be doing Tantra, sensual erotic massage and breathwork. I ran an ad offering sacred intimate work on the Internet, and I was shocked when most of the people who contacted me, primarily men, wanted me to dominate them! Giving sensual, erotic massage felt easy and natural to me, but BDSM was very, very challenging. I had to look deep within myself to even consider the possibility.

To discipline someone from a conscious, loving place is very different from unleashing anger.

I began to think of this work as "shadow work." By "shadow,"

I generally mean those actions and feelings that are considered taboo or not genteel—too ugly to talk about. Eventually, I began to explore shadow work, and as a consequence, I went deep into my own process. I had to face and integrate my own shadow, which was my unexpressed anger and frustration. I had to learn to accept and understand that part of myself, because I knew that if I acted unconsciously it could become dangerous. To discipline someone from a conscious, loving place is very different from unleashing anger.

Through my work, I've learned a lot about myself—a lot about my anger. The anger in me used to come out only when I was really backed into a corner. I was raised in the southern tradition that dictates that women are never, never supposed to be angry. A good southern woman has a lilting voice. She's kind, bubbly, entertaining and always has a big smile. A good southern woman is always sweet. So I sat on my anger until a series of interesting events educated me and helped me to embrace the rage inside of me.

I was twenty-eight, sick, terribly overweight, and exhausted. I had fybromyalgia and chronic fatigue. I was stuck in my life, and I was stuck in an abusive relationship that put me in the hospital twice. One day, I saw an ad for auditions for a play. The play, written and produced by Dr. Sharon Mathis, was about a woman who was torn between the needs of others and being true to herself. In a search for herself, she goes into the underworld, through hell, to be reborn. It was my story! It was perfect! I don't really understand how I mustered the energy, but I decided to go to the audition, and surprisingly, was cast in the role of a woman who, at one point, embodies the great Hindu goddess Kali. Going to that audition was completely out of character for me, and how I was cast in that role was a mystery.

Kali is an awesome, powerful, triple goddess. I was weak. All through the rehearsals, the director kept saying, "You're not projecting. We can't hear you. Can you express more anger? Is that all you've got?" But I was afraid of my anger. I didn't understand it. It was too big. It felt dangerous! I felt that if I let out my rage, I'd hurt somebody. Finally, the director pushed me so hard that I broke through my wall of fear and suppression, and I really let her have it! When I did that, everybody watching literally stood up and applauded. The director was astonished. When she asked, "Can you do that again?" I felt so free and I said, "Shoot, I can do that for the rest of my life!"

It was so good, so empowering! I felt so alive. I had been poisoning myself with my own stuffed anger. That was the very first time I had fully expressed that kind of energy, and in that moment, my life changed completely. In that moment, I went from feeling half dead to feeling fully alive, and I began to get well.

As I began to get well, I began to search for a better way to live, a very different way than I had known in the past. I threw myself into studying with a Native American woman who teaches the Lakota tradition. She guided me on my path toward wholeness, which included soul retrievals, and I totally turned my life around. I began to feel vital. I became a raw vegan, and I lost seventy pounds in about seven months!

Most importantly, my heart, my mind and my body exploded open all at once. It was an embodied spiritual awakening. I had the awareness of being filled with loving, ecstatic energy—no different than erotic energy. I felt the energy flow through me, through everyone and everything. I opened myself up to a higher power, and I came to understand that I am a consort to spirit. Now I understand that my primary relationship—a tangible, physical relationship—is to spirit. When I first had this awakening, I thought, "Oh, this is what it means when nuns speak about being married to Christ!" This union of spirit and erotic energy within me has been very healing, and because I know this so well in my own being, I feel I can help others become aware of this in their own bodies. Erotic energy is big, and it's important to be clear that the energy doesn't come from me; it flows through me.

> *...my primary relationship—a tangible, physical relationship—is to spirit.*

My work is healing work, very different from what you might usually think of as domination. I'm integrating light elements like Tantra, sensual massage and breathwork with shadow elements, creating a powerful path to healing that I call "Shadows and Light." When we lock away parts of ourselves we believe to be shameful, unacceptable or unlovable based on the messages we get from the world around us, we can become fractured—split. When those "unlovable" parts remain hidden away in the shadows, we're not whole—we're split. If we deny the complexity of who we are, we're walking around with only a portion of our power. We're not all that we can be in the world. If we can go into the shadow realm and reclaim who we are in our totality, we can become more powerful.

As individuals and as a planet, we are sick, we are in pain, because we feel split within ourselves and separated from everyone and everything around us. The key to our healing, to healing the planet, is in realizing our connectedness—the connectedness of all our facets, of body and spirit, of self and other, and of self and environment. Erotic energy is something that connects us all and connects all living things. Plugging into the erotic flow dissolves the feeling of separation faster than any other thing I've found. Penetration of the body can be penetration of the spirit. We could not do the things we do to ourselves, to each other or to the planet if we truly felt connected. If we can find our way back to knowing this connection in our lives, we'll find ourselves living in a different world.

I believe that when people come to me looking for forbidden pleasure, they are looking to venture into their shadow. My job is to guide them into that often scary but compelling place. To do that, I have to be grounded in compassion and love. I also need to be able to make a deeply intimate connection, a bond of trust with my clients. Because my clients know that I care about them, that I'm taking them by the hand and leading them safely through their experience, they don't feel victimized. They feel loved. It's all about intent. This kind of experience is often extremely erotic while being cathartic and healing. That level of intimacy, that deep sense of connection is what allows people to surrender to such profound experiences. Blasting through the barriers to intimacy is what sacred intimate work does. It gets energy moving in a big way.

Many of my clients are successful, powerful men who have to be in charge all the time. They come to me simply because they want the opportunity to let go of control for a while. It's a huge turn-on for them to have someone else dictate to them what they must do. They have a longing to be soft, to surrender and let me take charge. I believe it's a longing to embrace the divine feminine within.

I've worked with a few women, and I feel that because of my healing journey, I have a lot to offer women. I hope to work with more women, but historically it has been men who have sought out alternative ways to have their needs met. One of my goals is to create groups to help women access their inner warrior and really get in touch with their power. I want to help women to quit sitting on their rage, because it's such a source of vital, powerful energy.

One of the most powerful experiences I've had was with a man who I'll call Paul. Paul, who has a doctorate in psychology, came to me to do shadow work with a clear intention and a clear understanding of the healing potential of shadow work. He was an attractive man with a lot to offer, but he just didn't have confidence with women and wanted to work on that. In our sessions, we created a number of different experiences during which I dominated him, but I began to sense that Paul needed something else. So I consulted with another sacred intimate, John Ballew, and asked Paul to see him. After one session, John offered a powerful insight, which was that this man had rejected some aspects of his masculinity. John suggested that Paul could really be empowered by being dominant over me.

> *I want to help women to quit sitting on their rage, because it's such a source of vital, powerful energy.*

Normally I wouldn't allow myself to be submissive, but because I had worked with Paul for a while, I felt that I could really trust him. With Paul, I knew that it would not become a session of him releasing his anger in any way that would put me in danger. It would, in fact, be a real challenge for him to take up his power and be in command.

In our next session, I presented a specific list of things that I could agree to so that the boundaries were clear. I allowed him to tie me up and take control. He was completely in charge of how much pleasure, how much sensation, I did or did not receive. He was free to stimulate, tease, ignore or deny me as much as he desired. That work shifted something big for Paul. It was pivotal for him, totally life changing, and it's a happy-ever-after tale! Paul went out of town shortly after that session and met someone that he's now engaged to. He told me that he never would have had the confidence to approach this woman had we not worked together as we did.

Maybe we can just embrace our longings, our passion in a way that simply asks, "What is it that my soul hungers for?"

Paul had rejected a part of himself. His upbringing taught him that being assertive was being aggressive and that was bad, so he denied and lost an important part of himself. It was like throwing the baby out with the bath water. Consequently, he had lost a lot of confidence. When he reclaimed that part, he was able to take up his power in a very positive way. Paul hasn't felt the need to see me again. That's the bittersweet side of my work. I get to help people open to their longing, heal their wounds, and take up their power. I become very close to my clients, and when the work is really effective, I get to say good-bye.

I'm faced with a lot of judgment from people who don't understand my work. Sometimes that's a struggle. But my clients tell me that I've helped them to open their hearts, to breathe deeper, to learn how to relax and let go. I really feel good about what I do. My biggest concerns are about how my work affects my close relationships. I recently came out to my mother. I was in a relationship with an older man, and my mother was concerned that he would be controlling. She was afraid that I would be submissive to him. I assured her that I was not submissive and then I told her about my work. I held my breath because I didn't know how she was going to take it, but she was actually very pleased—kind of tickled! In the South, where women are taught to be submissive, my mother was actually delighted to learn that I could be so assertive.

Thomas Moore, who writes about the "longings of the soul," inspires me. His teachings help me to be with people and to be with myself without judgment. Our desires aren't wrong or bad. We're just wonderful, complex jewels full of light and dark and colors, and maybe we can just love that in ourselves and others. Maybe we can just embrace our longings, our passion, in a way that simply asks, "What is it that my soul hungers for?" The deepest longing of my soul is to return to the place of our origin where, I believe, we are all connected, we are all one.

Collin Brown is quiet, direct and precise — a regular guy doing not-so-regular work. In 1992, Collin bought The Body Electric School from Joseph Kramer and served as its director for 15 years. As owner, director, and workshop leader for Body Electric, Collin knows the potential for erotic energy to be healing and transformative. When I asked Collin to talk about his vision for this work, he told me that he's not on any sort of a mission. He doesn't have a grand plan or a big vision, just a passion to make the world a better place. Collin's ongoing work with Body Electric and his new work as a life coach supports individuals as they learn to access their own unique gifts and express them fully. I asked Collin to talk about his understanding of the nature of erotic energy. He has obviously given this much thought.

PHOTO CREDIT: FRANK ROSS

Collin Brown

Erotic energy is the energy that flows through the root chakra. It is the root. It's the foundational energy channel, and if you can get that activated, it tends to move up, activating everything else. It affects all the other chakras, and it's amazing what can happen when erotic or sexual energy starts to flow. In most of us, this energy is blocked for many reasons. There are layers upon layers, upon layers of stuff that we've attached to erotic energy. It's all tied up with romance, naughtiness, weird pornography, shame and abuse. It's tied up with serious fears about not being loved, fear of God, and fear of physical punishment. It's complicated. People have even been put to death because they dared to be sexual, so these fears are deeply planted in our collective psyche. It's these fears and myths about our erotic energy that keep us from getting but a tiny, tiny piece of what's possible. If we could begin to experience erotic feelings and just let go of the taboos of our cultures, we could allow this infinitely powerful energy to flow. It seems that we are both overly charged by all of these taboos (the forbidden is titillating), and at the same time, our capacity to be receptive, to really feel erotic energy, is diminished by that charge. We've buried the experiences of erotic energy under layers and layers of all this weird stuff, so how can we relax into really receiving and really feeling?

Imagine — you could have the most delicious, yummy, orgasmic tsunami come through your body and not even be having sex!

The Taoists gave us a way to regard erotic energy as pure and separate from all the unhealthy sexually charged junk, and it's not complicated! You can stimulate powerful erotic energy through simple tools like touch and breath and movement. It's revolutionary and ancient at the same time. You don't even have to focus on sex to get this energy flowing. It's amazing! You can have a full-body orgasm using only your breath, and the bonus is that breathing is not risky behavior! It's even legal! Imagine—you could have the most delicious, yummy, orgasmic tsunami come through your body and not even be having sex!

People come out of Body Electric circles or sacred intimate sessions exclaiming things like, "That was the most incredible orgasmic experience I've ever had!" or "That's the most amazing thing I've ever done in my life!" Most people only equate eroticism with having sex; genitals to genitals. But there is poverty in that kind of thinking, when people can reach incredible heightened states of awareness through breathing. This is what I'm exploring. These tools of transformation can be so simple. It can be as simple as focused, deep breathing.

Breathing gets people out of their heads and wakes up sensations throughout their bodies. What most people do is sedate themselves by chronically under-breathing. As a culture we tend to be shallow breathers, because we've been taught that it's not okay to have a lot of feelings. So the way to control feelings is to not breathe deeply. When we breathe more, we feel more alive. This is powerful medicine! What happens when people start to breathe is that they begin to have feelings, and they don't know what to do with those feelings. They often have a sense of losing control. It can be very uncomfortable, even scary, for people who are beginning to feel more acutely. They may feel nauseous or they may feel pain or fear after a lifetime of suppressing.

I'm different from a lot of people who might be seen as having a mission. I don't have a big specific plan or vision. I don't have that grand way of thinking. I have a few things I've figured out and I play with that, then I watch it unfold into something way bigger than me. I have a dedication, a commitment, to focusing on what feels meaningful in the world and what needs doing that isn't getting done. I guess that's my mission. There are many things I could be working on other than eroticism. I could be working to end poverty or to correct the way we've abandoned our teenagers or any number of other issues.

The thing that I am passionate about is personal freedom in all ways. I want to make it possible for people to be who they really want to be, and strangely, one powerful doorway to that seems to be Eros. When I lead sexual healing clinics, it's amazing how many issues in people's lives get activated. It's amazing how the heart, the psyche, the spirit gets activated. It's a hologram. If you open up erotic energy, then all the other important things come through. It's true, I'm focused on the erotic which is the root, but it's so much bigger than that. My approach in the world is holistic. If we commit to focusing on the whole — mind, spirit and body — then we must not leave out the genitals; we must not leave out Eros. For that reason, I have to focus on Eros, because everyone else is leaving it out. My apparent focus is on Eros, but I'm really more interested in the whole.

Whether I'm teaching an introductory class or a class for sacred intimates, I'm aware that I'm being a sacred intimate to my staff and a sacred intimate to the entire circle as well. I weave a container of heart energy that allows people to look inside to find what will feed them, nourish them, and give them some insight about their lives. Knowing what it is that moves me — what makes me feel really alive and wakes up my heart—helps me to stimulate others to activate their hearts. What often amazes people when they venture into this kind of erotic exploration is how activated they feel in their hearts. The love piece gets really charged. I think it gives us a startling perspective on just how shut down we usually are—shut down and detached from ourselves. It's so amazing to see what happens when the heart opens; not the least of which is that you get to be connected to yourself! From that place people can truly resonate and connect with each other. What we are all seeking is kindness, unconditional acceptance and connection. I want to create a container where we can peel away the layers of judgment, so that we look at our differences and recognize that our differences allow us to be human. We are different and that doesn't have to keep us apart.

The genesis of the idea for training sacred intimates came from Joseph Kramer. He created the term and started the training during the last year he owned Body Electric, which was 1991. The idea was to help bring greater consciousness to what happens between two people who are working together erotically, but it has a much broader context. So many people have come through the training who are not interested in teaching or setting up a private practice, but rather in having a very personal experience. The training can be a very powerful experience regardless of what you're going to do with it. There are so many ways that the idea of sacred intimacy

> *...friends could be sacred intimates for each other. Friends could simply touch friends and not be afraid of touching.*

could have an impact on the world. People get fixated and think it's all about sex work, and that is one version of it; but only one. Sacred intimacy can be as simple as holding someone while they cry. The big picture, the ideal, is that friends could be sacred intimates for each other. Friends could simply touch friends and not be afraid of touching.

There are many facets of a person's existence that this work can affect, and I don't pretend to know when someone is ready to step into this work or how it should affect their life. It's deeply personal, soul journey work. Through sacred intimacy we can explore what it means for a very wide range of people to be more erotically present in their lives. Musicians, therapists, body workers, teachers, physicians, even priests come to know that the erotic is so much more than what we typically identify it to be. It's so interesting. I talked to a therapist after a Body Electric workshop, and he told me that as a result of his experience, he now feels more erotically alive for his clients. It's not that he will be touching his clients, but he feels more alive, more present, more loving. I talked to a musician who described being able to find his muse through opening so deeply. When we open all of our chakras, including the root chakra, the erotic energy flows, and it can be a powerful creative force.

In spite of my deep belief in the positive power of this work, I'm not trying to take it out into the world. I don't want to have to go up against any number of organizations, like the religious right or many in the therapeutic community who would be threatened by our existence. I try not to argue with people who throw out objections to what we do. If it goes against everything in someone's personal pantheon of reality, then they certainly should not come — stay away. I'm just offering it so that those who are trying to find it can find it. Everyone's invited, and people come when they're ready.

It's very funny to me to think that my first venture into this arena started way back when I was a senior in high school. I was asked to serve as the male student representative on a board called the Citizen's Social Health Advisory Board in San Diego. It was part of the San Diego city school system. We reviewed all of the materials that the sex education teachers used in the city schools. We had a rabbi, a Catholic priest and a minister (sounds like the beginning of a bad joke), a former PTA president, and a couple of students on the board. It all looked very conservative, but as it turned out, we were a very liberal bunch. The board made all the decisions the teachers wanted them to make. If anyone in this conservative town complained, the teachers would just say, "Take your complaint to the advisory board." They had the system wired. So, at seventeen, I was involved in creating sex education curriculum!

I trace the beginnings of my connection to bodywork back to a group in Boston called Aqua Viva. Aqua Viva incorporated a number of modalities including bioenergetics, psychodrama and art, with the intention of flooding the senses, and thereby breaking through restricting patterns. I was attending one of their retreats, and in the middle of it all, I was given deep tissue bodywork. It was the first time I had experienced anything like that, and I was just blown away. I could not believe that one person could give me the experience I had over the course of those two hours. The way the therapist connected with me helped me to open to and release very tightly held pain in my body, and that physical release opened me to a very deep emotional experience. It was exceptionally purging and cathartic, kind of like emotional laser surgery.

Having had such a profound experience, I asked the body worker what she had done to me, and she told me she used a modality called Postural Integration. She then told me that the creator of Postural Integration, Jack Painter, was actually coming to Boston the following week, so I arranged to see him, and ended up going to him for a series of sessions. Postural Integration aims to relieve the chronic tension or holding that we have in our bodies. These chronically contracted muscles turn into very dense tissue which holds people in weird, unhealthy postures. One of the things that happened to me when I went in for these sessions was that I felt very pleasant tingling sensations which I now call *ching chi*. This energy, *ching chi*, felt like electricity moving through me. Some people call this energy kundalini. I spent over a year working with Jack Painter developing a lot of my awareness of the bodywork and my body, and I became very familiar with this energy.

From Boston, I moved to California, the Bay Area, where I explored a lot of different things. I was involved with various organizations that were putting on spiritual retreats, and I discovered lots of different schools of bodywork, one of which was Body Electric. What drew me to Body Electric was my desire to work intimately with men. I was afraid, knowing that this was something that was going to create erotic energy between me and other men. Still, the possibility of really communicating about the erotic experience was very attractive. I had read an interview of Joseph Kramer, and

I remember thinking, "Wow, this guy is really talking intelligently about eroticism." Joseph was talking about how poverty stricken our erotic relationships are, because we've been taught so poorly about how to really connect erotically. That connection wasn't happening in any other forum. It wasn't happening in the bathhouses or in the bars. Even the men's movement wasn't talking about eroticism. It was a big, important missing piece—a big hole.

My first Body Electric workshop, in 1979, was a huge opening for me. I don't even remember exactly what happened. My brain can't remember the details. All I know is that my body was on fire. Again, it was the experience of *ching chi*. Many people who come to Body Electric and experience this amazing energy for the first time are afraid of it; it surprises them. I wasn't afraid of it. It felt familiar to me, so I knew I was going to be fine and I was able to open up fully to the powerful sensations. What surprised me was the ability to produce that *ching chi* or kundalini energy without pain, but rather with breathwork and the raising of erotic energy. With Postural Integration, the release that produces this energy comes from someone digging very deeply into the body, into the underlying fascia, which can be painful. With Body Electric, the heightened erotic energy produced the same cathartic, freeing results.

Most men are living with their root chakra quite open, but their

> *Most men are living with their root chakra quite open, but their heart chakra is shut down. ... For women, generally, the reverse is true.*

heart chakra is shut down. That's a much generalized description of the male paradigm. For women, generally the reverse is true. The heart chakra is open; the root is shut down. One way to describe what happens both through Postural Integration and through the erotic work is to say that the chakras are aligned and balanced. The heart and the root chakras are equally activated.

Joseph Kramer and I strengthened our bond through our mutual interest in vision questing. Joseph had done his master's thesis on vision questing, and I was just getting ready to go on a vision quest of my own, so I asked him if he was open to talking with me about it. I hired Joseph to be my guide for my quest. Carrying only water, I spent four days alone hiking the Lost Coast Trail in Northern California. When I returned, Joseph led a ritual with some of my friends and some men from the Body Electric community to massage me back into my body—grounding me. It was lovely. Because I had this close connection with Joseph, I was invited to assist at the next Body Electric event and, as they say, I never looked back.

> *...[it] is so interesting to me, so fascinating, is to see people dropping so much resistance and really showing up to be their glorious selves.*

In 1990, I started teaching classes, and when Joseph did his first intensive I helped him put it together. I was present for every new event that took us to another level, and I went deeper with the work every step of the way. It became a life commitment that allowed me to translate the principles of the work into my private life. It didn't start that way, but my commitment became more clear as I went deeper into the work and started to feel the call from some deeper place—the call to say "yes" to whatever needed doing. It took continuous engagement with the work to maintain that navigational system, that conviction, but the call was very clear.

That commitment and clarity also gave me the imagination that I could actually be in relationship with someone who really understood and supported me and the work. I let go of thinking that the solution to relationship was to find someone who might just tolerate it. Part of this is also related to my bisexuality. It became clear to me that I could no longer hide my sexual identity. That had always been a struggle. I'd be with a woman, and at a certain point when I felt I had enough closeness, I'd tell her I was bisexual. It would always throw the relationship for a loop. So what became clear through my work with Body Electric was that I needed to be totally open. I could no longer even imagine being with someone for whom my identity—an out, open erotic healer—would be an issue. It gave me the courage and determination to hold out for a life that could really work.

Part of the draw that is so interesting to me, so fascinating, is to see people dropping so much resistance and really showing up to be their glorious selves. I get that what's happening isn't just some temporary high, but a life-changing technology. The never ending, ever changing stream of fascinating people who show up to explore their own personal process is entirely compelling. I am drawn to be with them in their commitments. I really feel that I came to this work as a healer. That's my interest and I've learned so much about ways, which feel largely unknown in the world, to help open people to healing. That's part of the thrill for me—realizing that this is such unexplored territory in terms of the healing professions.

If you go to the village, you can't pick out the shaman. Only the people in the village know who the shaman is. I feel like I have that quality. In a way, I'm a closet shaman and, I suppose, a closet radical. It's not that I have a need to be different or to be on the edge. The thing that I have is a very strong need to make a difference in the world, and I'm not attracted to things that are already handled. So if I weren't doing this, I would look for what else it is that people are going to sleep on.

I don't want to be seen as this radical, wild and crazy guy. My lifestyle is pretty sedate and mainstream-ish, but I have my work that is wildly interesting and unusual. I'm really rather conservative in my personal life. People think that I'm going to wild sex parties all the time, because they see me in intensely erotic space when I'm teaching, but I really have a very big separation between my personal life and my teaching life. I'm a private person. If people ask questions about what I do, I tell them. If they don't, I leave out details.

> *I'm not one to make big predictions, but if I dared to, I would look down the road thirty, forty, fifty years, and see this work as being much more accepted.*

I'm not one to make big predictions, but if I dared to, I would look down the road thirty, forty, fifty years, and see this work as being much more accepted. I would see that erotic healing work is not something that gets people all upset. I would see, hopefully, having a positive influence on American culture that seems so body-phobic and so "eroto-phobic." We would have more and more therapists embracing the concept of erotic healing. There would be more and more therapists wanting to get out of their licenses so that they could touch people. The world would shift from body fear to body acceptance. Each of us would feel at home in our bodies, and we would be unafraid of each other's bodies. Our hearts would be open and we would really, really know love. The truth is so authentic when you feel it in your body.

Reclaiming Eros

Sometimes a small inner voice leads us to find healing we don't know we need and treasures we can't imagine exist. This was true for Bob Hampton. Bob's life appeared full and successful—even enviable. Then it got better. With a soft southern accent, Bob generously shared how much his life has been transformed.

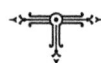

Bob Hampton

I've had a very, very good life. I grew up in the south. I would say I had a stable background with a typical all-American family. I was very involved in high school and college, with all the normal things of those worlds. Even though I knew early on that I was gay, I choose not to act on it until I finally came out in 1975. I think I escaped most, but certainly not all, of the issues and trauma that being gay invited at that time. Today it's very different, and though I still maintain a very private life—separate from my professional life—I don't hide my sexuality. I work in a corporate environment—in product design and development for some of the major mass marketers across the country, and I also do a lot of professional speaking and presentations. So, if I'm asked about my life, I'm happy to share, but I never make a big issue of it either.

> *Your father is the first person to validate you as a man. Being validated is such an important piece...*

I had very loving parents, and they were generally supportive, but I remember my father saying things like, "Stand like a man. Don't be a sissy." It was all verbal, but verbal criticism beat into a person's brain from an early age can be very troubling. Your father is the first person to validate you as a man. Being validated is such an important piece, and if you don't get the early validation, it follows you through life. Still, I chose to be who I was regardless of what he thought. I just didn't want to play baseball. Just recently, prior to my father's death, I had an opportunity to sit across from him in therapy and confront him about his words. He was levying the same troubling words on my nephew. I said, "From a very early age you called me those same names. Well, I managed to work through the hurt, to move on so when you look at me today, you see a fairly well adjusted man—a 58-year-old gay man. But I have to tell you, verbal abuse hurts. Words can be very destructive, and the words that you're using are the same words you used on me. This has to stop!" It felt so good to be able to say that to him.

In spite of my father's attempts to shame me into changing, I've pretty much stayed true to who I am, and I continue to enjoy my life fully. My work requires that I travel all over the world, which allows me to sample a lot of life's treats. I have always enjoyed massage, and I've had the opportunity to try many different styles of massage. About ten years ago I was in and out of Atlanta, Georgia, a lot for business. As I often did when I traveled, I searched the web for a good, relaxing massage and I found Ian Ellington's site. Well, I probably visited that site at least ten or twelve times and I remember thinking, "Oh my gosh! That sounds a little bit 'out there'. What does *sacred intimate* mean? What does *conscious breathing* mean? What does *Tantra* mean?" He had long hair, kind of hippie-like, but it all sounded very intriguing. It looked like it would be much different from a normal massage experience, so curiosity won and I finally booked an appointment—a two-hour session. I got there and we sat down—me on a sofa, him on an ottoman facing me and we just began to talk. He's a very easy, very comforting person to communicate with. He created such a safe space that I immediately felt very comfortable with him. He asked me about my intentions and then he talked a little bit about conscious breathing—this was different indeed! I told him, "I don't really have any major issues. I have a great job; a great life. I'm just interested in bodywork and Tantra. I read your bio and I'm intrigued." So we started with some synchronized breathing before we eventually progressed to the massage table. I was totally amazed that as I fell into the breathing and followed the breath, I reached new states of erotic feelings, but an unusual sense of peace. I found, even in that first experience, the conscious breathing opened up blockages I didn't even realize I was holding onto. So much of what we learn about sex we learn at a young age. We learn to masturbate quietly. We do it quickly so we don't get caught. We learn to breathe very quietly or hardly at all. So, simply learning to breathe expansively and feel safe when you're aroused can be a big experience. It can send you into orbit.

I continued to see Ian when I was in Atlanta, and we had some amazing sessions. Then he suggested that I look into some group experiences, and because I trusted him so much, I decided to give it a try. I attended a week-long workshop Ian held in California. The workshop was titled "Stepping Out of Your Sexual Identity and Into Your Sexual Power." I read the description of the workshop and something about it really resonated in me. We were asked to bring an altar object and we were invited share a bit with the group about the significance of the object. I brought a bracelet—a very simple bracelet given to me by my lover, Jim, who had died several years ago from a brain aneurysm. I had met Jim when I was twenty-five, and we were together for eight years before he died. Our relationship was incredible, and I struggled for many years trying to get back on track after that loss. To have had that, at such an early age, and then lose it—that was something! Sometime during that workshop I realized that even though Jim had died many years ago, I never totally let go. It's not that I hadn't ever addressed losing Jim—I had. But clearly I had more to do, and in that kind of setting, things have a way of resurfacing so that you can deal with them in much greater depth.

During the workshop we explored many powerful exercises. We took simple risks like standing in front of each other naked and placing our hands on each other's hearts. I know this sounds kind of odd, but this simple act of allowing such vulnerably and sharing acceptance was enormous.

> *We took simple risks like standing in front of each other naked and placing our hands on each other's hearts.*

There was one particular exercise that really had a major impact on me. This was a "Yes and No" exercise. We took turns asking a string of questions, and no matter what the question, we were told to answer "yes." Then we asked and were asked the same questions again and we answered "no." During the third round of questions we answered honestly "yes" or "no." The exercise was repeated again, but this time it was physical. We were asked to offer or ask for some kind of touch. It could be any kind of touch—sensual, erotic or something as simple as a foot rub.

The receiving person would then answer honestly, "Yes, that touch is something I want." or "No, I don't want that."

Prior to that week, I had been very much a "yes" person. I always found it easier to be agreeable rather than risk causing hurt or confrontation. I was an "under-the-radar" kind of guy—it was safer. With these exercises I learned to take a hard look at what really serves me and what doesn't. I practiced being real about what I want or don't want. I got very real—found my voice in a big way—I shouted. Man, it felt good, and making that exercise physical really set it deep into me. I learned that I could stand the consequences of being honest even if it meant I disappointed or caused someone to turn away from me. I learned to set confident boundaries and expectations for myself as well as for others, and I've been able to hold onto that. What's really great is that I've been able to apply this to my business as well as to day-to-day personal events.

> *I learned that I could stand the consequences of being honest even if it meant I disappointed...*

After that workshop I took a hard look at what I really want out of my life. Now, I'm not a guy who believes that you have to be in a relationship to be totally full, but I realized that I had spent a great deal of my life running away from that possibility. I had stayed on the move, running from one job commitment to another to avoid getting close to anyone and risk being hurt. It's been very easy to make excuses and say, "Oh it's my job." But, honestly, I do control my life and I do control my schedule (to a certain extent). So, one of the intentions I've set for my life is to stop the running. I've made huge changes. I still have to travel quite a bit, but I've created more of a home base so that my life is no longer contained in a twenty-seven inch suitcase.

It's so easy to get off track, forget what we really want and forget that we have the power to make life be what we want it to be. So many times we just get muddled down with, "I wish, I wish." Each of us has needs, but we're often afraid to ask for what we want, either because we think we won't get it or because we're afraid we will.

Since that week in California I've attended a number of events. I have to say that I'm in the best place I've ever been in my life, and I credit a great deal of that to the work I've done in individual sessions with Ian as well as in groups with men who are so willing to be open. It's been very, very powerful. I have deep friendships that go back 35 years, but the men that I've met through this work share a bond unlike anything I've ever known. There's something special about the honest vulnerability and acceptance that we shared. Thank God that I made the leap into the unknown, and thank God I didn't do it half way. I showed up fully for what so many people might perceive as crazy.

At this point in my life, there is nothing more powerful and nothing I can do better for myself than to do this type of work. There is nothing that grows me spiritually, mentally or physically more than exploring, in an empowered way, erotically. If I hadn't taken a chance and booked that first appointment with Ian, I could have looked back and said, "Yes, I had a good life." But, now I feel that my life has been magnified and enriched. To some people this all sounds so crazy. To that I say, "Well, you just have to experience it." I'm a firm believer that if you always do what you've always done, you'll always be what you've always been. Change is a good thing. Risk is a good thing. Thank goodness I found this.

I feel so much healthier inside. I never considered myself unhealthy, but now I have so much more passion—for everything. I have been in the same career—design—my whole life. I was fortunate, from an early age, to know what I wanted—to know my talents and really push myself to learn everything I could. I also did everything I could to promote myself and develop great connections in the design world. My work's been featured in national magazines. You could say that I've built a very big name within the industry, so I'm asked to present at industry conferences. I've always had a lot of enthusiasm and enjoyed the public speaking, but five years ago I grew very tired of my work. I could just slap something together and everyone thought it was wonderful, but I knew I was stale. Up until then I might have attended some big design expo to try to motivate myself, but through my work with Ian, I've

I made eye contact and felt connected—human to human. It's a small thing, but it makes a difference...

found a tremendous resource of energy. I'm just more alive and motivated. Now, when I'm speaking, I hit the stage with more pep in my step and I'm communicating much better. Enthusiasm and creativity just pours out of me, and I know it's because of opening up erotically.

It's hard to overstate just how different I feel. I've always been an outgoing person, but now I'm just over the top. I'm more aware and open to people I meet in simple everyday encounters. Recently, while checking a bag at the airport, I took time to acknowledge the attendant. I made eye contact and felt connected—human to human. It's a small thing, but it makes a difference in how I feel, and I'd like to think it makes a difference to others. I just find life a lot more enjoyable.

Bob Hampton

Empowered choice is the core mission of Betty's work. When I first met Betty she was running a conference for ASEP (Association of Sexual Energy Professionals) in Phoenix. I was immediately impressed by her confidence. She was friendly, easy, and not pushy, but clearly in control of this large group of very independent people. Betty walks her talk in all facets of her life. When I interviewed Betty for this piece, she was working on her book, closing in on the final rewrite. Betty told me how the length of the writing process had taken her by surprise and how much emotion was extracted by the writing process. We had much in common.

PHOTO CREDIT: HAWK JONES

Betty Martin, DC

Pleasure is a physiological/emotional process with a purpose. It's the way our bodies, our brains and our bio-chemistry respond to certain experiences. Pleasure brings a physiological change which can have an effect on the way we perceive ourselves and each other. Science is clear on this. It's no longer a question. When you have pleasure with someone, the changes in body and brain chemistry basically make you fond of each other. This is why pleasure can be a bonding process between people. This is the purpose of affection.

Pleasure can also make you feel emotionally vulnerable, and emotional vulnerability can also be bonding. When you see each other's deeper "heart," you are naturally more bonded. Think of a time when someone revealed something tender to you and you felt closer to them.

Sacred intimacy? This was not a part of my career plan. I grew up in a conservative, military family. It was an affectionate family—healthy by comparison. I grew up in the 50s and 60s with the idea around sexuality that girls weren't really "supposed to." My job as a female was to keep the men around me happy and at the same time say "no" to being sexual, and at the same time be as attractive as I could possibly be. No one ever said that of course. It just seeped in from the culture. Then the 60s hit—good news or bad news—depending on how you look at it. For me it was good news. I became aware that there was another way of looking at things, and once that door opened it never closed. Since then, my life has been about exploring and questioning everything. I'm always curious and always want to explore things deeply and intensely. That's just who I am.

I went to Chiropractic school and worked in that field for about thirty years. I just loved it—loved being in the healing arts. After you have your hands on thousands of people, you begin to notice things you might not otherwise notice. During those years I was also learning, practicing and teaching peer counseling and other kinds of body-mind integration modalities, so I became very fluent in the interplay of emotions, body, mind and spirit.

Then, in my early forties, realizing that my erotic life was a big mystery to me, I decided to attend a workshop, a Body Electric workshop for women; it opened a whole new world to me. I found out about this workshop from a friend. It appealed to me because it was an area of my life that I was curious about but knew very little about. It promised to be experiential—not a lecture, and it was for women only. That was helpful. It was a place to start. If something else had come along I probably would have started there, but I'm very grateful to have stumbled and landed where I did. Several things happened at that workshop that really opened me up. Things that seem simple and quite ordinary to me now were big steps at that time. We stood naked, daring to look at each other's bodies. We were vulnerable, dancing for one another. We heard each other's stories of erotic histories and we gave each other ritual erotic massages. I had never before seen women in so much pleasure and let me tell you, it was astoundingly beautiful. I was humbled, inspired, deeply touched, and awed. It was all a huge stretch for me, but it was also profoundly healing. All of my concepts about sexuality, eroticism, desire, relationship, intimacy, and love had once fit so predictably, but by the end of that workshop they no longer fit the same way. It was as if they had all been torn into little bits, thrown into the air and landed

> *I discovered that my sexuality lives in my body, belongs to me, and it's like rocket fuel...*

in a different pattern.

The most critical thing I realized was that my sexuality belonged to me—absolutely and completely. Most of my life my sexuality had been in response to someone else's desire, because I was taught that that was my job as a female. I discovered that my sexuality lives in my body, belongs to me, and it's like rocket fuel—for my use in whatever way I choose.

For a number of years, exploring that revelation became a spiritual path, and I was fortunate enough to have a handful of friends who were on similar journeys, so we explored together. Like most people, I had grown up in a culture where sexuality and physicality were presumed to be the opposite of spirituality. Supposedly, the more spiritual a person was, the less interested they would be in sex. What I found when I began exploring intensely physical experiences was that the more attentive I was to my physical experience and the emotions that came with it, the more spiritual an experience it felt like. I experienced feeling states of being in blissful connection with the universe; feeling states of deep forgiveness, compassion and love for myself and for others. I experienced a willingness to look at reality in a way that had nothing to do with theology or cosmology but rather just feeling what it was to be conscious in that moment. People talk about having consciousness-expanding, out-of-body experiences. If you

> *People talk about having consciousness-expanding, out-of-body experiences. If you really want to be radical, try an in-the-body experience.*

really want to be radical, try an in-the-body experience.

For a long time I recognized that the physical and the spiritual worlds were related, but now I realize that they are the same thing. Now, "spiritual" is a word I rarely use because I'm not sure how it's any different than anything else. To me it's all the same. In communicating with people, it's sometimes helpful to use these words, but in my experience and how I live my life, the split is gone. It's very clear to me that one of the most potent spiritual experiences I can have is to be completely in my body and accept reality in this moment. I'm not even sure if I can tell the difference between emotional and spiritual either. It's all part and parcel of being human.

Those years of exploring were some of the sweetest years of my life. We would spend a day or weekend together and each of us would have a turn receiving attention from the others. When it was my turn, I might have 3, 4, 5 or even 6 people supporting me in my experience. I might ask to be held, to talk, or to engage with someone in a particular sensual or erotic way. The intention was for me to be attentive to my own experience and what I needed for my own heart. This was indescribably rich on many levels, and I'm inexpressibly thankful to have had that time. It changed the course of my life.

For most people, any kind of erotic activity is assumed to be "having sex," which is assumed to be intercourse. So when I tell people we were exploring erotically, most people assume that we were "having sex." What was actually true is that we were exploring Eros in a whole different way. We were looking at arousal as a state of consciousness. We were asking, "What's my inner experience when I'm in an aroused state? What are the possibilities and limits?" It wasn't about hooking up. It was outside what most people would consider as being sex. There's a big difference between Eros and sex. I think of Eros as an underlying, prevailing force that runs through all of life, and I think of sex as something more to do with genitals. You can have an erotic experience that has nothing to do with your genitals, and you can have a genital experience that is not at all erotic.

During this period, I was still practicing Chiropractic, and word got out that I was comfortable talking about sexual experiences. People began to look me up because they needed someone to talk to. At the same time, I realized that I was using my hands in healing service, but I was interested in bringing more of myself, more of my body into that service. I needed to learn more about doing that.

I went to a training for Sacred Intimates where I met several traditional sex workers—prostitutes. I was so touched by their hearts, their presence and the descriptions of some of the work they did with people. I was very moved by the ways in which they were deeply supportive of people's experiences. For myself, though, I held onto a certain streak of self congratulatory propriety and primness. Then I went to visit a friend, also from that work, in New York. This woman did a very traditional sexual massage—rub and tug. No chakras, no Sanskrit words, no fancy folderol, no theology—nothing—just a great massage and hand job. I worked with her for a few days, and I was touched by the value of that service. It didn't have to be enlightening. It didn't have to be life changing. It didn't have to be even particularly healing. It was just a wonderful and needed service to offer, and I was struck by the tender ordinariness of it. It got me over my primness about sex work.

At some point I felt ready to offer experiential sexual healing. I closed my Chiropractic office and opened a completely different office. It was a bit scary—a leap of faith—but my heart was no longer in practicing Chiropractic. My heart was elsewhere, and when you have your hands on people, they deserve to have your heart there too.

My first Sacred Intimate practice was based on a very therapeutic model. I wrote my brochure and designed my website in a way that would be accessible to therapists and married people. That was my approach. I did careful assessments. I taught empowerment, touch and communication skills—all experiential—all clothed. It was very satisfying work. What surprised me most was that an awful lot of people had extremely narrow views of what Eros was about and settled for very mediocre sexual experiences. People felt restricted on what was possible, but their hearts were aching to find freedom.

My background as a Chiropractor greatly influences my work and how I think. I have deep respect for the physical/emotional interplay. I have a sense of healing as a phenomenon; how sweet, precious and valuable that is. My training and experience have helped me to hone my ability to notice what's true about the person in front of me. I think that's my strong suit. When I started working as a Sacred Intimate, I realized that people walked in my door with very different levels of readiness—very different skills. If I just put everybody through the same process, I would be doing a great disservice. I needed to assess where they were before we decided where to go.

After a couple of years I decided to work more explicitly with some people—people who seemed to be ready for that. So I opened another branch of my practice in which more directly sexual experiences were sometimes possible. I guided and accompanied people through sensual, sexual and erotic experiences, and I went with them. I interacted with people in astonishingly intimate ways — intimate both bodily and emotionally. When appropriate, I could be generous with my own body and experience. I didn't just tell them how to do it and send them home. This kind of guidance required me to be very aware of their emotional, physical and mental states and needs. It wasn't easy. It took a lot of care and attention and I just loved it! This is the path of the "Sacred Whore." It is a calling.

Through those years coaching and being intimate with hundreds of people, I learned some things. Most importantly: how central and crucial it is to be in touch with what you want and how to communicate it. That's not news. What was news was seeing just how poorly most people do so and how unaware they are about where they slide into compliance. Most people, myself included, have an amazing ability to go along with what we think is expected. If you want to notice what you feel and what you want, you have to slow down. I've asked countless numbers of people, "How would you like to be touched right now?" and I've gotten a lot of blank stares from that question. People say things like, "I don't know. No one has ever asked me that before" or "I don't know. I'm usually the one giving." If you are unable to know what you want and say it, you're stuck. There is nowhere to go except where someone else wants to go. So as a Sacred Intimate, I could have a bunch of wonderful, fun things to do to people, but the most important thing turned out to be teaching empowerment. It's liberating and life changing. It is also, I have come to see, a spiritual path. This has become the heart of my work and now the focus of my book.

I've been and continue to be my own laboratory. During the years I was teaching, I was also learning from my own struggles at home. With my lover, I began to see how convoluted our communication was. We would be in bed and I would wonder, "Is he doing this for him or is he doing this for me?" Then I would think, "This is not what I want. I'd like something else right now, but if he's doing it for him, I'm okay with it. I'm happy to give it to him. He's apparently enjoying it, but knowing whether he's doing it for him or doing it for me makes a difference about how I feel about it and whether I want to go along with it." I was afraid to ask, so we went for years like that. That's a common story for couples—afraid to spoil the mood, so you don't ask. Instead you spoil the relationship.

The ability to both give and receive and to tell the difference between the two is not as predictable as most people think it is. It's not about who is doing what to whom but more about who is giving the gift. Our ability to receive a gift of affection and attention is the substance that everything else grows out of. When it's difficult or uncomfortable to receive, we avoid it; we might try to give instead, which means that our giving is not really giving—it's avoiding our own discomfort. It's only by learning to honestly receive that we are able to clean up our giving. A big part of learning to receive is learning the difference between receiving and tolerating. Real receiving is first about acknowledging that you have a desire; slowing down enough to know what the desire is. Then you can learn to receive by taking in a small amount of what you want so that you're not overwhelmed by it. You don't learn to receive by pushing yourself. You can't try harder and relax into receiving at the same time.

As I've become more aware and fluent in asking for what I want in my erotic life, I've also become clearer about what I want in the rest of my life. I've become more aware of how my desires, my choices and my empowerment affect my community and my world. I take my desires more seriously—really own them, acknowledge them, and deeply consider how they affect others and whether I have consent. This is so important to me. I feel that I also have to consider desire and consent in my choices about what I buy and what I consume; what I consent to by virtue of paying my taxes.

> *I've become more aware of how my desires, my choices and my empowerment affect my community and my world.*

Some years back I was pondering an event that had happened between me and my lover. He had done nothing wrong. It was just another one of those convoluted communication and consent mix ups. Still, I was troubled by it—had never been able to find resolution to my feelings. It was really haunting me, even years later. Then I realized—wait—the reason I can't make myself feel okay about it, can't make myself accept his reason for the breach, no matter how hard I try, is because there actually is no reason good enough for doing something to someone without their consent. It's not that his reason was not good enough; it's that NO reason is good enough; absolutely none. Obvious? Perhaps, but it's one of those things that hits you. It shook me to my roots.

Then right on the heels of that came another realization—doing things to people without their consent is the basis of our entire civilization. We stole this continent without the consent of the existing population, we enslaved millions and we still do in less obvious ways. That very year we were bombing villages and imposing our will across the globe. If we really owned our desires, respected the desires of others and insisted on consent, we could no longer do that.

I'm working on a book, *The Lover's Touch: How to Bring Your Heart into Your Hands* and "Lord have mercy," it's a lot of work. Interestingly, it's the inner work, my personal process, that's been challenging. Writing the book itself is not that difficult. The subject matter—desire, intimacy, clarity and consent—is stuff that is very dear to me; we teach what we need to learn. But all of the heartbreak and mixed feelings that surround that topic came up when I started to write about it. Then came the belief that women are not supposed to know the things I know, and that if they do know they are not supposed to tell, and if they do tell they're not supposed to tell straight out. They're supposed to tell with some sort of cute humor—be a nice girl about it. Then I was overwhelmed by this amazing feeling of fear of just talking or writing about any of this stuff at all. All of that is completely irrational, of course, because there's nothing all that radical in my book. It's simply a new way of looking at things. The fears were way out of proportion to the project. Still, the fears were there. I think women carry a certain collective fear, and maybe it's when you speak up that you feel it most acutely. I have written and rewritten more versions than I can count.

Now I'm actually getting close to writing something that I think will be useful. I think in a few months it will be ready.

My work evolves. It has a life and an intelligence of its own. I'm no longer offering the sexier end of the erotic work. It just doesn't interest me. I've learned to listen to what my body says and if she says, "I'm not available for that anymore," I have to honor her. I need to be very clear about what I'm willing to do and what I'm not willing to do, or I have nothing authentic to offer — no joy. So, I'm focusing on what one of my colleagues refers to as the "dry work" rather than the "wet work." It's imperative that I bring my own awareness to this work, and that changes with time. It changes for everyone. Recently, a friend said, "Betty, you are in a committed monogamous relationship with your book right now." She's right. I've also recently said, "My cunt is on a silent meditation retreat." Maybe my body will be interested again once my book is done. I don't know.

So many people give up all forms of affection when they can't or don't want intercourse any more. What a pathetic loss!

There's a question that women will often ask about age, menopause and desire. Women will often say that with menopause they lose desire, but I don't think that's true. There's a big piece missing. If you think the only desire that counts is the desire for sex and if you think the only kind of sex that exists is the kind you've always had, no wonder you don't want that. When a person says, "I don't have any desire," I don't believe it. You have a desire for *something*. The task is to find what that is. So we are back to that core piece—noticing what you *do* want. So many people give up all forms of affection when they can't or don't want intercourse any more. What a pathetic loss! There's just so much more. This is not only true for people as they mature but also for young people as they awaken to Eros.

A great part of my work has been to help people slow down, notice what it is they actually want—not what they think they are *supposed* to want—and really enjoy that thing, no matter how small, mundane or weird they may fear it might be. Then they learn to trust themselves, and they naturally become curious about what else they might like. It goes back to the physiology of pleasure. You can have pleasure in a very relaxed state, and pleasure in an excited state, and we all have our comfort limits within each of those. But for pleasure to occur, there must be certain changes in brain waves, blood and brain chemistry. It's not a theoretical state. It's real physiology. When you push yourself, trying hard to like something that you really don't want, or something that's too much of what you do want—you will not find that physiological response. Effort and bliss, hard work and pleasure—the brain cannot do these at the same time. The trick is to take a few minutes with something that you honestly enjoy and just enjoy that—really enjoy that. You might get more pleasure out of a four-minute foot rub than an hour of working hard to *try to* enjoy a full-body, erotic massage. Once you do find that relaxing response, your heart will naturally

> *Effort and bliss, hard work and pleasure—the brain cannot do these at the same time.*

expand and your body will want to explore.

What captures my heart most these days is working with other sex workers. I just love coaching, mentoring and training other practitioners. When I first started practicing, I didn't have a mentor—someone to model after, so I made more mistakes than I might have. For example: I'm quite comfortable being naked. It's not a big stretch for me, but most people have assumptions about that. In the first week of my practice I learned that if you don't want people grabbing for it, don't uncover it. As I became clear about my intention, about what I was offering, I learned to describe and present it more specifically. I got fewer inquiries and fewer clients, but the clients that I did get were ready for what I was offering. I'm hoping to help others make fewer mistakes—learn from mine and what I've discovered. I am passionate about teaching those things that make sex-work practices professional. The assessment skills, slowing down to notice, teaching them how to teach their clients empowered choice—the basics.

Over the years in my exploring and in my work, I have occasionally wondered if this realm, the sexual and all its relations, is really an important pursuit. To be worthy, doesn't it have to be something spiritual or take people to some new dimension? I no longer worry about that. As humans, we have a natural capacity to enjoy and connect with each other. This impulse to care for one another and express our affection is so precious. It's our nature. For that reason alone, it's worth doing. If you can bring ease and joy to that, that's good enough. It doesn't have to be "cosmic." It just has to be real.

Betty Martin, DC

Emaya is a delightful combination of the quintessential wise woman and curious child. She is an ever-energetic teacher, visionary and word artist. Perhaps Emaya's greatest gift is her ability to focus her attention on a concept and then, with her soft German accent, articulate it with such clarity and poetry that your entire being attends. Whether she is speaking to one person or weaving a sacred circle with a large group, it's obvious that she was born to teach; she just can't help it! I have had the sweet privilege of spending many hours with Emaya both as a student and as a friend. She has taught me and inspired me. It's no wonder Emaya is often invited to bring her pearls of wisdom to places as far away as China and Ireland.

PHOTO CREDIT: CAROLYN DAVEY

Emaya

As a little girl in Germany I played freely in the wild. I moved through my childhood being very connected with the trees and the animals. I did not have too many taboos imposed even though I was raised Catholic. I enjoyed a kind of paradoxical freedom. I remember that my mother would say things like, "Sex feels good. Don't tell anybody I told you so." Or when the priests in our village were known to be having relationships with women, my mom would say, "Well, they're men first." She really had an instinctual knowledge about the importance of sex and a great generosity of spirit. She would also say things like, "Prostitutes are very important women. Just don't be one," or "Oh, so what if they're gay, that's fine." I count her as one of my good influences, but of course there are other influences, and so I did feel very conflicted. I got the message that being sexually explorative or liberated as a married woman was okay, but being single required a different standard. I got that from the nuns, not from my mother. She was fun.

I remember that my mother would say things like, "Sex feels good. Don't tell anybody I told you so."

That conflict became most acute when I was in my twenties. At that time, my sexual explorations were driven by an unhealthy need and desire to be loved. I misunderstood what it was to be loved. I had a lot of sex, and it was an interesting game to explore, but ultimately I decided it wasn't a very good game for me or for my young daughter. It seemed like I was wired into a pattern of attracting men who were abusive. I couldn't imagine being in a relationship with someone who was kind. I had a lot of fun, don't get me wrong. It was just bad for me.

So, when I was thirty, I took a vow of celibacy. It was discovered that I had cancer cells on my cervix as a result of an STD that I had contracted. I felt very guilty about that, but I began to wonder, "What does this cancer have to teach me?" Weighing everything, I decided to remain celibate for a year, and actually I remained celibate for most of my thirties. I wanted to distance myself from my habits and see what I was using sex for. It seemed very clear to me that I was being sexual without consciousness or intentionality—I just did it. Those years of celibacy were one of the most interesting periods of my life. I learned a lot about myself, including how I had objectified men; not really seeing them as human. During that time, I read Betty Dodson's work and explored self-pleasuring, which became a very satisfying alternative. I became happily sexually autonomous.

Later, I was almost amazed to find that my daughter had grown up. Ten years had gotten by me—ten years of celibacy! I decided that everything was fine. I could grow old with my connection to spirit and nature and my self-pleasuring practice. Perhaps, I'd have an occasional cosmic wow with someone. Then suddenly, I was about to turn forty and I thought, "Holy cow, I'm going to be forty. Who am I sexually and erotically? What's going on?" It was completely astonishing to me. I was forty! I wasn't in a relationship. I wasn't lusting after anyone, but I did have a certain *joie de vivre*. I was in love with the world. I didn't feel any internal need to be with anyone. I felt erotically free, but somehow, it disturbed me that I didn't have a regular partner. Somehow, I felt odd in a world where everyone was striving to be coupled in some way. I wondered if I was sexually repressed or if there was something else wrong with me. So there I was, at a pivotal point in my life with lots of questions.

I needed to shake things up and search for some answers, so I sold all of my belongings and took myself to South America for two months. It was a wonderful experience. That began the period of my life that I refer to as "the time of *cuntscious* exploring." While I was there, I had a really wild affair with someone. It was thrilling, but I didn't fall in love with that person. I decided that when I got home, I would just try to carry on as I had before. Since I had sold everything, including my car, I had to do a lot of walking. I had quite an interesting experience one time while I was walking. I had this absolute sense that some being of light was walking next to me all the time. It was a very beautiful, exceptional feeling and it was also a very erotic feeling. So I thought, "Well, something is going to happen!" The very next day I saw an ad for an erotic workshop for women. I signed up and I went!

The workshop was very experiential, experimental, and radical. It was my first erotic experience with women, which was scary, profound and liberating. Even though the teachings of my upbringing were quite open, it was still an experience of breaking major cultural taboos. To be touched by and to touch women, to be naked and sexual in the presence of others, and to be so honored by others, rearranged my cellular structure in a way that left me with a new feeling of freedom in my body. It was a feeling I had long desired, but until now, I had no idea how to get. I didn't feel like I had to give myself a label of any kind. Just because I had an erotic experience with women didn't suddenly make me a lesbian, nor was I a heterosexual woman, nor was I bisexual. I just had this amazing, satisfying freedom of floating in an erotic sea. That experience changed

The result of my exploration is that all of life is erotic to me.

everything. It shifted the way I massaged people. My senses were more alive. I also felt like I became more kind. I felt at ease with the rainbow of different gender expressions. I even felt more relaxed around my daughter.

From that point I started exploring Tantra and Taoist expressions of eroticism and sexuality. I very intentionally put myself into circles of experimentation, and through this vehicle found a lot of wonderful friends. I love the fine commitment to honesty, while being erotically expressive, that I find among these friends.

The result of my exploration is that all of life is erotic to me. It's such a beautiful way of looking at the world. I've let go of my inner tension around arousal and all the rules about being a woman. Now I feel free to be turned on all the time. Now I have total freedom of choice, and I am in charge of my behavior. It's quite liberating—very healing. I can make very conscious choices about who to engage with and who not. I can choose this experience or that. I feel more generous and more understanding toward myself and others about all expressions of consensual sex. It's ridiculous to have imposed restrictions on erotic expression. It's crippling to the spirit.

As I became more relaxed in my own body, I became more acutely aware of the intense suffering that is brought about by ignorance

> *As I became more relaxed in my own body, I became more acutely aware of the intense suffering that is brought about by ignorance around sexuality.*

around sexuality. When people feel secretive or scared or tense about the erotic flow in their bodies, they suffer. But really, it doesn't take all that much to help them relax with it. One of my biggest desires is to help people help themselves. Whether I am working with individuals or couples or groups, I want to educate them. It's what I call "erotic literacy." I want to create a field of permission, a field of safety, where they can know what it feels like to let go of some of the old restrictions. I want to say, "Here is the banquet. Here are some possibilities. You get to choose. You get to say 'yes' or 'no.' You get to change your mind."

I believe that life with conscious Eros is immensely important. It lets folks taste life in their bodies. With this experience, they are much more likely to notice and connect with life in others of the same species and with all the life on earth. Our work, erotic energy work, helps that process. It is good and sacred work, and we need to support each other in doing it. We need to do it excellently and articulately so that it can be translated for those who haven't experienced it; so that it can be presented as the natural and sacred thing that it is. If people just want their jollies, that is fine, but maybe more ordinary venues would suffice for that. Our work is for those who are really interested in combining Eros with heart and mind to serve the unfolding of life and to be a connecting force that is awake and present. I have watched and touched bodies for many years now, and

> *I believe that life with conscious Eros is immensely important. It lets folks taste life in their bodies.*

I am convinced that cultivating an increasingly friendly attitude toward the body, and therefore toward incarnation and life itself, is totally worthwhile work.

When I think about what is important, I think that the first task as a human is to surrender to incarnation. We have to realize that we are here in the body, and really, truly, we don't know what's after that. As far as I know, here and now is where it's at. Everything else is speculation. I'm in my body. I don't know about reincarnation, and frankly, I want to get here first. We've got to get here; we've got to get grounded; we've got to breathe; and we've got to be kind to each other. Kindness is a very high form of human evolution. That kindness needs to extend to erotic and sexual expressions toward self and others. We need to be committed to speaking our truths in a loving way, making sure that we really understand and respect each other. Basically, I believe that we have to open to the erotic energy in our lives and learn how to behave with it. It all seems so simple, and yet it's apparently very hard to do. That's the crazy-making thing.

> *...I think that the first task as a human is to surrender to incarnation.*

I often think of my work as that of a translator and mediator. I feel that can I help folks become a little more literate about their erotic world, and then help them translate their experiences so that they can connect with others in a more satisfying way. I try to instill powerful concepts that are essential to surviving in the community of life on earth. Learning respect for choices in the moment, witnessing, grounding and breathing are not only useful for erotic encounters, but also for creative living on all levels. When these concepts are embodied down into the pelvis, it makes for a felt and lasting experience with enormous possibilities. Even if folks don't immediately put what they've learned into practice, something shifts on a cellular level for them. Maybe the shift for these people comes from the experience of surviving a taboo breach or two in the open witness of community. Maybe it's the heart connection and humanizing experience of acceptance and deep sharing with folks they wouldn't socialize with in their everyday life. I think of all the lovely faces that I see in my private work and in the groups that I work with, and I feel so privileged to be a part of their lives.

I also think the work we do helps people in relationship find their way into an intimacy that is inclusive of sacred Eros. Our work helps couples keep their erotic interest alive in new and creative ways. Too many times people fall into numbing, unconscious patterns or even use sexuality to hurt one another, and sometimes they just don't know any better. Our work opens up dialogue and presents possibilities that a lot of folks haven't thought of before. It gives them the opportunity to become conscious of and to increase their choices of behavior with one another. This is good.

Kindness is a very high form of human evolution.

Periodically I become afraid as I notice how much cultural tension there is around sex and how personal sexuality is often used as a weapon to embarrass or even destroy people. All around us is a generally negative attitude toward the body and sex. People seem to be afraid of freedom and generally still seem to gravitate toward suffering rather than happiness.

Just a couple of years ago, I found myself seriously questioning why the hell I would be doing this work. Then I found myself in the center of one of the best feeling, most loving circles I've ever had the privilege of leading. From the straightest, squarest guy to the wildest sadist, this circle had a huge range of erotic expression and an unparalleled open-hearted acceptance. The feeling of fun loving curiosity and generosity is so memorable that I am still feeding myself with it as a possibility of life on earth. I think the vibration created by a circle like this will continue to be felt and attach itself to the network of light-minded beings that span the planet.

My intention for myself is to keep offering erotic education for people in all forms, whether it's hands-on through body experiences or teaching or counseling. I'm also writing, but I have this problem about writing because I feel like it's all been said. There are so many smart, wise people that I've read and been fed by. So many people have devoted so much love and attention to erotic health and the connection between the genitals and the heart and the mind. It's all been done, really. For me, the task is just to collect this information and to spread it out in my own unique way.

So, where do you go from here?

If you've read this far into the book, something must have impressed you, inspired you or provoked you in a significant way. Maybe you had a few 'Ah ha!' moments. Maybe it will be enough for you to spend some time thinking about what you've read, or maybe you want to process some things with a friend or your therapist. Maybe you want to seek out a Sacred Intimate or sex worker to explore with, or maybe you want to find a retreat where you can explore Eros in a group environment.

If you decide to take the next step and work with someone like the people in this book, please keep a few important things in mind:

- **Choose carefully.** Whether you're hiring a sex worker, an electrician, a doctor or a hairdresser, remember that all fields have gifted practitioners and quacks. Buyer beware. The word Tantra is often used to raise the price of a sensual massage. A sensual massage can be quite wonderful and it may even be healing, but it's not Tantra.

- **Ask for references.** A good way to find a sacred intimate is through a personal recommendation from someone who has experienced his work. A sacred intimate **should not** be willing to give you the names of her clients, but you should be able to gather information about her from other practitioners. Ask for credentials. Find out what he's studied; what training(s) he has taken. Ask if she works with a supervisor or peer review, and find out who that is.

- **Trust your feelings and your intuition.** Follow your instincts. If you see red flags, heed them. Your intuition is more accurate and valid than any expert in the field. You are in charge of you. If you take only one thing away from this book, take away the certainty that your body, your sexuality and your erotic experience belongs to you.

- **Consult with a psychotherapist.** If you are currently working with a therapist, let her know you plan to explore Sacred Intimate work. If your therapist has not heard of Sacred Intimate work, but is open-minded, you can suggest that he read this book.

- **Ask questions.** Ask about anything that doesn't seem clear, that you don't understand or that makes you feel uncomfortable. Notice if you feel like you are being heard, honored and answered.

- **Set boundaries.** Be very clear about what you want and what you don't want. Your boundaries should be honored without question or judgment. Remember that you can stop a session, change it, or even leave. Your SI will have boundaries as well. Find out what's offered and what's not. Ask about confidentiality. This should be a given, but it's always worth mentioning.

- **Set intentions.** Articulate your desires and intentions for the session. A skilled practitioner can help you clarify your intentions. She may ask you to fill-out an intake form to help both of you understand what your intentions are. You may simply want to create a session of being seen and heard. It's not necessary to have a huge physical experience. Some of the most powerful sessions happen when you express yourself and you are received without judgment.

- **Breathe.** Nothing happens without breath. Erotic energy is like fire. It cannot ignite without air. Get plenty of it. Conscious breathing is essential to expansive erotic experiences.

- **Check in with yourself.** Stay aware of how you are feeling. Are you breathing easily and consciously? Do you feel comfortable and safe? Is the session going too fast? If you're not comfortable with the pace or progress of the session, say so. Ask for what you need.

- **Be gentle with yourself.** Erotic exploration can be transformative, and transformation can be messy. You may experience very intense, sometimes uncomfortable emotions. You may feel upset or confused. Make sure you have some way of dealing with issues that arise. Find a good, wise friend or an open-minded counselor. Be tender with your experience. Be mindful about how you share that experience. Leave out the information about who did what to whom. Those details often sound odd out of context, and sharing could tarnish your experience. Leave the details private. Share your feelings.

- **Tap into your resources.** Information provided in the glossary and reference sections of this book is intended to help you begin to navigate your way through the world of sacred Eros. It is not a complete list, but rather a sample of possibilities. The internet will provide much more. If you are lucky enough to live near a friendly sexuality boutique or toy store, stop in. These stores can be great resources.

Whatever you decide to do, wherever this adventure takes you, celebrate your precious journey. Life incarnate was meant to be delightful. Enjoy it! Claim it! It's yours.

Glossary

BDSM: Bondage and discipline (BD), sadomasochism (SM). Each is a specific variety of erotic power exchange under the general rubric of SM.

Big Draw: A process used to induce an altered state of awareness in which healing, transformation and transcendence can take place. It has roots in Taoist and yogic techniques. It starts with a series of charging breaths (deep, rapid breaths to build up oxygen and energy in the body), followed by the retention, then slow controlled release of the breath.

Bioenergetics or Bioenergetic Analysis: A form of somatic psychotherapy that combines psychological analysis, work with the body, and relational therapeutic work. The approach recognizes the importance of the body-mind connection to psychological development and emotional health. Bioenergetic Analysis was developed by Alexander Lowen, MD, as a modification and extension of Wilhelm Reich's work.

Body Electric School: The Body Electric School (BES) teaches body-based healing arts that recognize and utilize the holistic connections between body, mind, spirit, and Eros. BES conducts workshops designed to help people experience the full potential of self and others through touch, conscious breath, movement and honoring the wisdom of the body.

Bondage: The practice of being physically restrained as a means of attaining sexual or other gratification.

Breathwork: The use of breathing patterns to induce altered states of consciousness for transcendence or transformation. Breathwork can be used to explore emotional, physical, and spiritual realms of one's psyche. Includes various techniques such as Rebirthing Breathing (developed by Leonard Orr) and Holotropic Breathwork (developed by Stanislav Grof). Breathwork is often used in conjunction with the Big Draw.

Chakras: A Sanskrit word meaning wheel. Chakras are thought to be energy centers of the human body located vertically along the spine, at and above the crown of the head.

Chi (also **Qi** or **Ch'i**): In traditional Chinese culture chi is the essence of any living thing. Qi is frequently translated as "energy flow," and is often compared to notions of prana, pranayama or mana. The literal translation of "qi" is air, breath, or gas.

Curandero (or **Curandera** for a female): A traditional folk healer or shaman in Hispanic America. Curandero is translated as "healer" from Spanish.

Cunt: Though in America this is considered a derogatory term for a woman's genitals, the word derived from the great oriental goddess Cunti or Kundi, the Yoni of the Universe. Related words include kin, cunning, ken, knowledge, learning, insight, remembrance and wisdom.

Doula: A person, usually a woman, who provides support to pregnant women and their families during labor, birth, and postpartum.

Fybromyalgia: A syndrome characterized by chronic pain in the muscles and soft tissues surrounding joints, fatigue, and tenderness at specific sites in the body. Also called fybromyalgia syndrome, fibromyositis, Fibrositis.

G-spot: An area inside the vagina that is extremely sensitive to direct pressure. The spot is called the G-spot, or Grafenberg Spot, after Ernest Gräfenberg, MD, the first modern physician to describe it. When properly stimulated, the G-spot swells and leads to orgasm in many women. It is sometimes called the Goddess Spot.

HPV (Human Papillomavirus): A group of viruses that are infectious and can cause a range of symptoms including genital (and non-genital) warts. Most cases of cervical cancer are preceded by HPV infection.

Kali: Sometimes referred to as Kali Ma, or the Dark Mother. Kali is the Hindu triple goddess of creation, preservation and destruction, in recognition of the complete cycle of life required for Earth's sustainability.

Kegel Exercises: Exercises designed to strengthen and tone the pubococcygeus (PC) muscle in the pelvic floor. Originally developed by Dr. Arnold Kegel in 1948 as a method of controlling incontinence in women following childbirth, they have been found to increase sexual enjoyment and erotic response in both women and men.

Kinsey, Alfred Charles (1894 – 1956): American biologist and professor of entomology and zoology. Kinsey founded the Institute for Sex Research at Indiana University in 1947, later known as the Kinsey Institute for Research in Sex, Gender, and Reproduction. Kinsey's research produced the Kinsey Reports and the Kinsey Scale. Though highly controversial in the 1940s and 1950s, his work opened the door of the study of human sexuality and has deeply influenced modern cultural values.

Kundalini: Energy that lies at the base of the spine until it is activated, as by yoga, meditation, erotic stimulation, or other spiritual practices. Once activated, it moves up the central channel, or spine, of the body. From Sanskrit, kundalini has been compared to *chi* and *prana* in other practices.

Mantra: A Hindu term referring to a sacred word or phrase which is repeated in prayer, meditation, or chanting with the intention of invoking the power of sounds. Most are salutations of God in His or Her various forms.

Microcosmic Orbit: A breathing technique designed to move one's energy through the meridians of the body, popularized with this name by Mantak Chia. A similar technique is used in some yoga practices.

Movement Therapy: Movement therapy refers to a broad range of eastern and western movement practices used to promote physical, mental, emotional, and/or spiritual well-being.

PC Muscle (Pubococcygeus Muscle): The pubococcygeus muscle runs from the pubic bone to the coccyx in the human pelvis. It supports the genitals and other organs in the pelvic region.

Postural Integration (PI): A somatic therapy developed by Jack Painter. The uniqueness of the PI method lies in the simultaneous integration of deep tissue myofascia reorganization, breath work, body movement and awareness, as well as emotional expression.

Psychodrama: A psychotherapy method developed by Jacob L. Moreno which attempts to restructure dysfunctional behavior and thinking. It is a method of psychotherapy in which clients express themselves through dramatization and role playing. Using both verbal and non-verbal communications, scenes may be enacted to depict memories, unfinished situations, inner dramas, fantasies, dreams or intentions for the future.

Rebirthing Breath or **Rebirthing-Breathwork:** A therapeutic modality developed by Leonard Orr which is used to heal suppressed emotions such as anger, fear, and sadness, etc.

Sadism: Pleasure or sexual gratification derived from inflicting pain or emotional intensity on another person. Named after Comte Donatien Alphonse François de Sade, known as the *Marquis de Sade* (1740 – 1814).

Shadow: The unconscious, repressed or hidden parts of our personalities. Dr. Carl Jung claimed that "Everyone carries a Shadow, and the less it is embodied in the individual's conscious life, the blacker and denser it is. At all counts, it forms an unconscious snag, thwarting our most well-meant intentions."

STD (Sexually Transmitted Disease): Any of a number of diseases, including Chlamydia, genital warts, gonorrhea, herpes, syphilis and others, that are usually contracted through sexual intercourse or other intimate sexual contact.

Tantra: A Sanskrit word meaning "weave," it is also translated as "getting closer" (tra) to "self" (tan). Tantra, thus, means connecting or interweaving soul or spirit with one's physical existence. Various techniques, traditional and modern, are used to achieve spiritual transcendence through physical means. Tantra as practiced and taught in America usually involves sexual techniques.

Transpersonal Psychology: A form of psychology developed in the twentieth century arising out of work by Abraham Maslow (1908 – 1970) and others. Encompassing a wide variety of practices and tenets, the principles common to them are that the human has the ability to transcend personal ego and human conditions to reach higher potentials and states of consciousness, including spiritual and transcendent states.

Vision Quest: A rite of passage in some Native American cultures. Usually undertaken with the guidance of a tribal Medicine Man or Woman, it can include fasting, solitude, physical challenge, and/or ingestion of natural mind-altering substances. This quest is traditionally undertaken for the first (or only) time in the early teenage years, often as an initiation into one's place in the tribe.

Vulva: The external female genitalia, including the labia, clitoris, and vaginal opening.

Yoni: A Sanskrit word used in the West to indicate any or all of the female sexual organs: the womb, vulva, vagina. It is translated in various ways, including "holder," "place of birth," "source," "Divine Passage," "sacred temple," "fountain," "home" and "holy well."

Resources

*The information that follows
is by no means an exhaustive list, but it can
get you started on your own journey.*

ALEX JADE, MSW, is an erotic educator, sacred intimate, and psychotherapist living in Seattle, Washington. She has mastery in experiential erotic education and the use of ritual as a healing tool. Alex's specialties are gender exploration, classical Tantra, and BDSM. Alex is on the faculty of The Body Electric School. She also teaches independent workshops nationally.
ALEXJADE@DRIZZLE.COM

AMERICAN ASSOCIATION OF SEXUALITY EDUCATORS, COUNSELORS AND THERAPISTS is comprised of members who share an interest in promoting understanding of human sexuality and healthy sexual behavior. WWW.AASECT.ORG

ANNIE SPRINKLE, PhD, prostitute/porn star turned performance artist/sexologist, has produced and starred in her own unique brand of sex films, photographic work, teaching workshops, and college lectures. She is an internationally acclaimed performance artist who tours with one-woman shows about her life in sex. Annie has championed sex-worker rights and health care. She was one of the pivotal players in the 1980's sex-positive feminist movement.

Annie's writings include her autobiography *Post Porn Modernist, Hardcore from the Heart: The Pleasures, Profits and Politics of Sex in Performance*. Her book, *Dr. Sprinkle's Spectacular Sex: Make Over Your Love Life with One of the World's Great Sex Experts* is her first mainstream how-to self-help book. Her current art project is The Love Art Laboratory (WWW.LOVEARTLAB.ORG). WWW.ANNIESPRINKLE.ORG

ASSOCIATION OF SEXUAL ENERGY PROFESSIONALS is a nonprofit collegial organization providing sexual energy professionals with educational and networking opportunities that inspire psychological, somatic, and energetic approaches to sexual wellness and sexual wisdom. WWW.GOASEP.ORG

BETTY DODSON, PHD, is the founder of the pro-sex feminist movement, an award-winning artist, author and sexologist. In 1972, she designed and facilitated nude Bodysex groups for women and the following year created the first feminist slide show of vulvas for the NOW Sexuality Conference. Her self-published book, *Liberating Masturbation: A Meditation on Selflove* (1974) was a feminist classic that was retitled *Sex for One: The Joy of Selfloving* in 1987. Betty has produced a number of instructional articles, books and videos. She has been featured in national magazines including *O Magazine, Glamour, Cosmopolitan, Vogue* and *Playboy*. She has also appeared on several talk shows, including The View. Betty's new memoir, *Betty Dodson: My Sexual Revolution* recounts her life and role in the feminist movement. Betty has partnered with Carlin Ross, focusing on sex information online at WWW.DODSONANDROSS.COM

Resources

Betty Martin, DC, a Chiropractor for 30 years, leads holistic, erotic education workshops for individuals, couples, groups and professionals. Her workshops focus on autonomy and empowerment in consensual touch and erotic play. Betty also trains and certifies facilitators for a boundary and communication workshop called Cuddle Party, which is a clothed, non-sexual event. She is currently writing a book called *The Lover's Touch*. **WWW.SACREDEXPLORATION.COM**

The Body Electric School is a school offering a variety of workshops that teach touch, conscious breath, and erotic wisdom. **WWW.BODYELECTRIC.ORG**

The Center for Sex and Culture provides non-judgmental, sex-positive sexuality education. **WWW.CENTERFORSEXANDCULTURE.COM**

Dr. Christian Northrop is an internationally known physician, awarding-winning author and speaker. She is a passionate proponent of medicine and healing that acknowledges the powerful role of the unity of the mind, body, emotion and spirit in creating health. Dr. Northrop is the author of two *New York Times* best-selling books, *Women's Bodies, Women's Wisdom* and *The Wisdom of Menopause.* Her latest books, *The Secret Pleasures of Menopause* and *The Secret Pleasures of Menopause Playbook*, focus on the importance of pleasure in creating joyous and vibrant health. Dr. Northrup has dedicated her lifework to helping women learn how to thrive by creating health on all levels. **WWW.DRNORTHRUP.COM**

Collin Brown is a holistic health practitioner who served for 15 years as the owner/director of The Body Electric School creating and expanding the school. A graduate of Harvard College, Collin teaches classes for Body Electric and is a life coach supporting individuals as they learn to access their own unique gifts and express them fully. His practice blends touch, breathwork and transpersonal psychology. WWW.DEEPERREALMS.COM

Easton Mountain Retreat Center is a loving community, retreat center, and sanctuary created by gay men. EMRC embraces and hosts sex-positive events for all genders and orientations. WWW.EASTONMOUNTAIN.COM

Emaya (Elfi) Dillon, RMT, has been a bodyworker in private practice for 30 years. She lives on Gabriola Island in Canada and is a faculty member of the Haven Institute (WWW.HAVEN.CA). In 2000, she joined The Body Electric School as a faculty member. Emaya created the Body Awareness Process, a "kinesthetic liberal arts intensive" in support of people reclaiming and expanding their erotic genius. Her classes are playful and reach deep into the heart of the desire to connect with life in our bodies and with each other. ELFIMAYA@SHAW.CA

Gay Spirit Visions pursues nurturing and healing heart connection between like-minded men. WWW.GAYSPIRITVISIONS.ORG

GINA OGDEN, PHD, conducted the first nationwide survey on integrating sexuality and spirituality (ISIS). She is the author of *The Heart and Soul of Sex: Making the ISIS Connection* and *Women Who Love Sex: An Inquiry Into the Expanding Spirit of Women's Erotic Experience.* Gina leads professional training and workshops internationally and has been featured on several radio and television shows, including *Oprah.*
WWW.WOMANSPIRIT.NET

Harper's Encyclopedia of Mystical and Paranormal Experience is a book by Rosemary Ellen Guiley, San Francisco: Harper Collins, 1991.

HUMAN AWARENESS INSTITUTE was founded in 1968 by Dr. Stan Dale, Doctor of Human Sexuality. HAI offers workshops dealing with intimate relationships and human sexuality.
WWW.HAI.ORG

IAN ELLINGTON After many years of working with women as an OB/GYN, Ian now works with men, couples and groups who are seeking personal transformation and growth. Ian is a somatic practitioner integrating Reiki, conscious breathwork, Tantra and Taoist modalities. **WWW.THEGARDENOFIAN.COM**

THE INSTITUTE FOR ADVANCED STUDY OF HUMAN SEXUALITY is the only graduate school in the United States approved to train sexologists. **WWW.IASHS.EDU**

Isa Magdalena is a certified sexological bodyworker, educator, and libido activist. Her journey has led her to discover the tools that facilitate the healing of the imposed split between sex and spirit, sex and life, body and soul, and sacred and profane. Isa facilitates individuals, couples and small groups in Taos, New Mexico, as well as across the United States. Isa is the author of *Full Spectrum Sex Libido: Where Sex, Science and Spirit Meet.* **WWW.LIBIDOMEDICINE.ORG, WWW.WOMENSORGASMPROJECT.COM**

John Ballew is a licensed clinical psychologist. He is a member of the American Counseling Association; The Association for Gay, Lesbian, Bisexual and Transgender Issues in Counseling; and the Society for the Integration of Spirituality and Psychotherapy. John is also on the faculty of The Body Electric School. **WWW.BODYMINDSOUL.ORG**

Joseph Kramer, PhD, founded The Body Electric School (1984), EroSpirit Research Institute (1993), and The New School of Erotic Touch (1999). He is currently Assistant Professor of Clinical Sexology at The Institute for Advanced Study of Human Sexuality in San Francisco where he teaches a professional course for sexological bodyworkers that leads to state certification. He has produced a collection of DVDs including *The Best of Vulva Massage* and *Uranus: Self Anal Massage for Men*. His commitment is to continue to train world-class somatic sex educators. **WWW.EROTICMASSAGE.COM**

Resources

Kenneth Ray Stubbs, PhD, is a certified sexologist and sexual shaman. Before becoming quadriplegic, he taught at The Institute for Advanced Study of Human Sexuality in San Francisco and led sacred sexuality seminars throughout North America and Europe. Ray has produced an impressive number of instructional books, DVD documentaries, and card sets including *The Essential Tantra, Erotic Massage, Women of the Light: The New Sacred Prostitute* and *The Path of the Sexual Shaman.* WWW.SACREDPROSTITUTE.COM, WWW.SECRETGARDENPUBLISHING.COM

Loraine Hutchins, PhD, author and activist, is a sexuality educator who inspires people to integrate the spiritual and the erotic in their everyday lives. WWW.LORAINEHUTCHINS.COM

Margot Anand is a teacher and writer who has played a major role in the growing popularity of the modern American variety of the ancient practices of tantric sexuality. Her books, *The Art of Sexual Ecstasy, The Art of Sexual Magic,* and *The Art of Everyday Ecstasy,* have sold in excess of a half-million copies. Anand has been teaching since 1970, and operates the SkyDancing Tantric Institute. WWW.MARGOTANAND.COM

Mark Michaels and **Patricia Johnson** have been teaching together since 1999. In October 2001, Dr. Jonn Mumford (Swami Anandakapila Saraswati) named Mark and Patricia lineage holders of the OM Kara Kriya Tantra system for the Americas and Europe. Mark and Patricia are the authors of award-winning books, *The Essence of Tantric Sexuality* and *Tantra for Erotic Empowerment.* WWW.TANTRAPM.COM

The New School of Erotic Touch, Dr. Joseph Kramer's school, assists people in learning the skills of pleasure and trains teachers of erotic touch and erotic education. WWW.EROTICMASSAGE.COM

Nut (pronounced "Noot") **Butterfly** is an internationally recognized Nubian-Khamite priestess, speaker and bliss activist. As chief priestess of Kra Mut Ankh ~ Temple of the Mother of Life, she is the holder of the lineage of Sh'ti Mer, a resurrected ancient Afrakan initiatory path of Orgasmic Alkhamy, and once-lost great-grandmother to Indian Tantra. Nut is a favorite guest on several national radio shows and is featured in Kenneth Ray Stubbs' DVD *Magdalene Unveiled: The Ancient & Modern Sacred Prostitute*. Nut shamelessly proclaims, "Orgasm Iz Enlightenment!" WWW.ORGASMICLIVING.COM

The Red Thread of Passion: Spirituality and the Paradox of Sex is a book by David Guy, Shambhala Publications, 1999.

Rudy Ballentine, MD, is a psychiatrist, holistic physician, teacher, author, and was the president of the Himalayan Institute (Yoga) for many years. Rudy has authored and co-authored books on nutrition, meditation, Tantra, breathwork, yoga and psychotherapy including *Radical Healing: Integrating the World's Great Therapeutic Traditions to Create a New Transformative Medicine* and *Kali Rising: Foundational Principles of Tantra for a Transforming Planet*. He studied for 20 years with a Tantric master, and leads workshops on Tantric sexuality for all genders and all orientations. LOBOVAL@AOL.COM

SACREDEROS.COM is a directory of erotic teachers and sensual healers, Tantra, and sacred sexuality. **WWW.SACREDEROS.COM**

The Sacred Prostitute: Eternal Aspect of the Feminine is a book by Nancy Qualls-Corbett, Inner City Books, 1988.

SELAH MARTHA is a sex educator for teens and adults with a private therapy practice for all genders and orientations. She is a trained facilitator for Our Whole Lives curriculum as developed by the Unitarian Universalist and United Church of Christ churches. **WWW.SELAHMARTHA.COM**

SEXOLOGICAL BODYWORK is Dr. Joseph Kramer's training for erotic educators who endeavor to assist individuals, couples and groups to deepen their experience of embodiment. **WWW.SEXOLOGICALBODYWORK.COM**

SHALOM MOUNTAIN RETREAT AND STUDY CENTER is a loving community offering retreats and private counseling for healing, health and transformation. **WWW.SHALOMMOUNTAIN.COM**

SHERI WINSTON, CNM, RN is a medical professional, sexuality educator, and author of the award-winning book *Women's Anatomy of Arousal: Secret Maps to Buried Pleasure*. She teaches classes and hosts webinars for people of all preferences, inclinations and orientations. Sheri is on a mission to transform our culture's attitudes about sex through education. She is the founder and executive director of the Center for the Intimate Arts. **WWW.INTIMATEARTSCENTER.COM**

Singing Deer, Sacred Intimate, poet and artist, holy woman, healer, teacher, Life Coach, and advocate is based in Atlanta, Georgia. She has been assisting people one-on-one and facilitating groups since September, 2001. **www.singingdeer.net**

Tantra.com is a wonderful resource for finding teachers, workshops and information about techniques. **www.tantra.com**

Wheels of Light: Chakras, Auras, and the Healing Energy of the Body is a book by Rosalyn L. Bruyere, edited by Jeanne Farrens, Fireside Publishers, 1994.

The Women's Encyclopedia of Myths and Secrets is a book by Barbara Walker, Harper Collins, 1983.

Acknowledgments

It was gratitude for the people who are opening the door to our vast erotic potential that first prompted me to write. To all of them, several of whom are featured in this book, I am deeply grateful. I give thanks to Margaret Wade for supporting this impassioned yet inexperienced writer through the first version of this book. Thanks to Lori Harley for her editing and design talent, and her patience.

There are others whose love, influence and guidance helped to see this project through. Thanks to Stewart who gently shoved me onto the road of this erotic adventure. Thanks to Kenneth Ray Stubbs, my mentor and guide. Thanks to Pam and Peter who convinced me to write with honesty and vulnerability. Thanks to Isa, my comrade in writing, who schlepped books all over New York City with me. Thanks to Meg, my soul sister, for seeing me through damn near everything. Thanks to Shalom Mountain and The Body Electric School and all of my community there for helping me open my heart. Thanks to my loving daughters, my sons-in-law and my grandchildren for giving me endless hope and joy; and thanks to Joanie, my proofreader, my best friend, my love and life partner, for walking beside me all the way.

~ **Suzanne**

About the Author

PHOTO CREDIT: JESSICA G. YOUNG

Suzanne Blackburn lives with her beloved partner, children and grandchildren in Maine where she practices and teaches Lomi lomi, Hawaiian healing touch. She also leads workshops on awakening to Eros and the sacredness of sexuality. Suzanne has written and published several articles on this subject. *Reclaiming Eros* reflects her commitment to living a loving, passionate and conscious life.

RECLAIMINGEROS@GMAIL.COM

CPSIA information can be obtained
at www.ICGtesting.com
Printed in the USA
BVOW06s0957170517
484383BV00020B/268/P